PARTS Iˢᵗ ENGLISH Part Viz ENGLISH EMPIRE containing yᵉ Articklands near Hudsons Bay New North & South Wales New Britain
na Carolania or Florida California, Sommer Iˢ Bahama Iˢ Jamaica & yᵉ CARIBY Iˢ II SPANISH

BAFFINS BAY

ARCTICK LAND

Hudsons Straits

NEW NORTH WALES

TERRA LABRADOR

HUDSONS BAY

NEW BRITAIN

NEW SOUTH WALES

NEW FRANCE

LAKE SUPERIOR

LAKE HURONS

LAKE ERIE

NEW FOUND LAND

The Main Bank

False Bank

Cape Cod

...ract of Land
...of Wild Bulls

SEA OF THE ENGLISH EMPIRE

Bermudas als Summer Islands

THE GOLF OR BAY OF MEXICO

BAHAMA ISLANDS

ANTILLES Iˢ

WEST INDIAN SEA

CARIBY ISLANDS

SOTTAVAN Iˢ

HONDURAS

YUCATAN

JAMAICA

...AIN

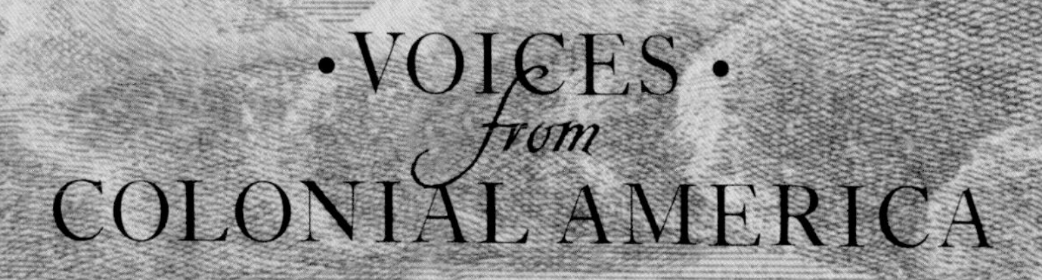

DELAWARE

1638–1776

KAREN HOSSELL

WITH

KARIN WULF, PH.D., CONSULTANT

NATIONAL GEOGRAPHIC

WASHINGTON, D.C.

For information about special discounts for bulk purchases, please contact National Geographic Books Special Sales:
ngspecsales@ngs.org

STAFF FOR THIS BOOK

Nancy Laties Feresten, *Vice President, Editor-in-Chief of Children's Books*
Suzanne Patrick Fonda, *Project Editor*
Robert D. Johnston, Ph.D., *Associate Professor and Director, Teaching of History Program University of Illinois at Chicago, Series Editor*
Bea Jackson, *Director of Illustration and Design, Children's Books*
Jim Hiscott, *Art Director*
Jean Cantu, *Illustrations Specialist*
Carl Mehler, *Director of Maps*
Justin Morrill, *The M Factory, Inc., Map Research, Design, and Production*
Priyanka Lamichhane, *Editorial Assistant*
Rebecca Hinds, *Managing Editor*
Elisabeth MacRae-Bobynskyj, *Indexer*
R. Gary Colbert, *Production Director*
Lewis R. Bassford, *Production Manager*
Vincent P. Ryan and Maryclare Tracy, *Manufacturing Managers*

Voices from Colonial Delaware was prepared by
CREATIVE MEDIA APPLICATIONS, INC.
Karen Hossell, *Writer*
Fabia Wargin Design, Inc., *Design and Production*
Susan Madoff, *Editor*
Laurie Lieb, *Copyeditor*
Jennifer Bright, *Image Researcher*

Body text is set in Deepdene, sidebars are Caslon 337 Oldstyle, and display text is Cochin Archaic Bold.

Library of Congress Cataloging-in-Publication Data available on request

ISBN-10: 0-7922-6408-8; ISBN-13: 978-0-7922-6408-8 (hardcover)
ISBN-10: 0-7922-6864-4; ISBN-13: 978-0-7922-6864-2 (library)

Printed in Belgium

Contents

Delaware COLONY

1755

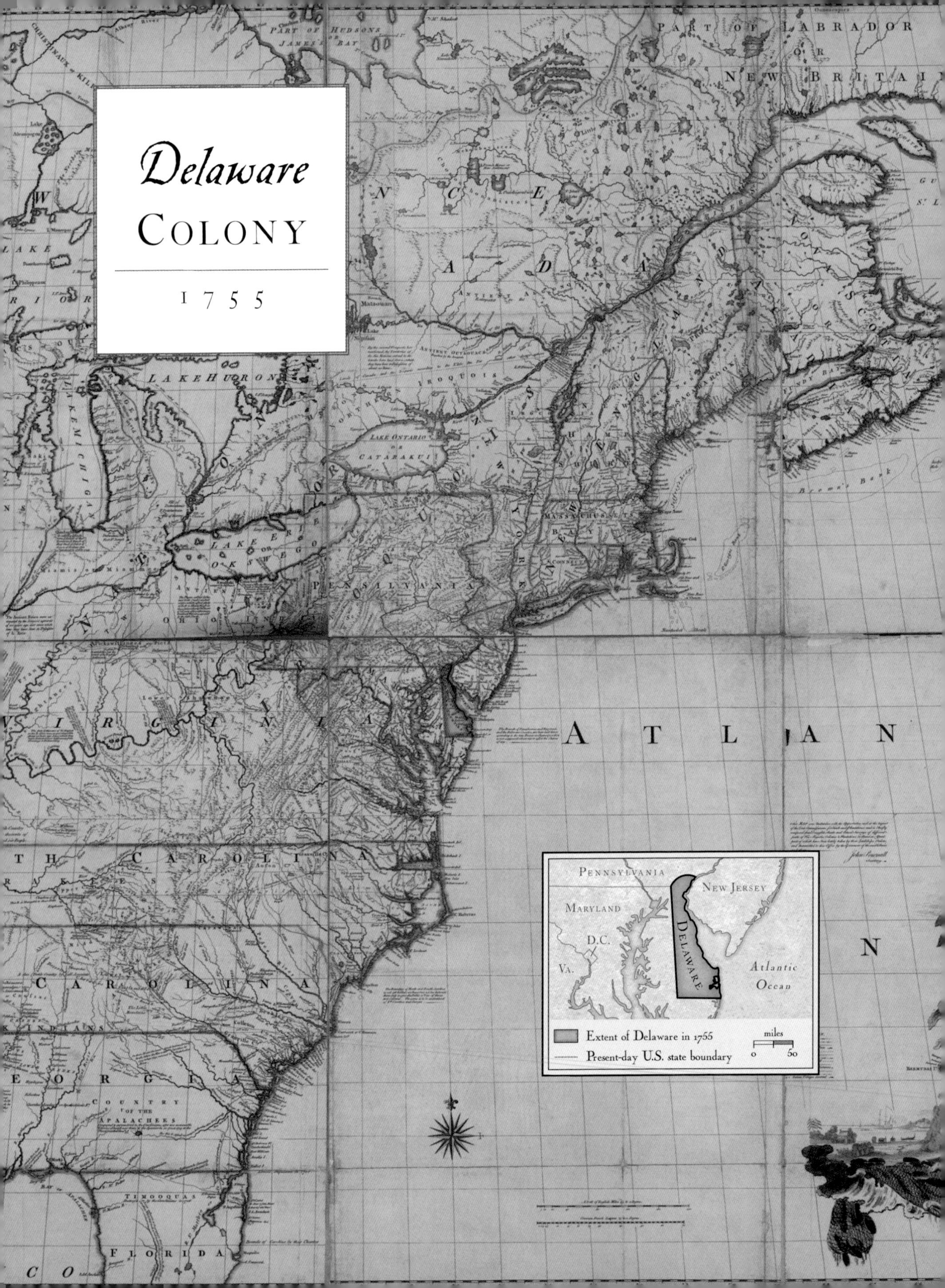

INTRODUCTION

by

Karin Wulf, Ph.D.

This 19th-century engraving by Benjamin Ferris shows Old Swedes Church, built in 1698 by Swedish Lutherans who settled Wilmington, Delaware. The church, still used for worship today, is the oldest church in the country that still stands in its original form.

The name "Delaware" comes not from native America, as do so many place-names on our continent, but from a governor of the English colony of Virginia. In 1610, an English captain and explorer, Samuel Argall, set out from Jamestown to investigate lands farther north. Happening upon the bay and the river, he named both for his governor. In 1776, organizers of the new state that was in rebellion against

OPPOSITE: The area labeled Delaware Counties on this 1755 map created by John Mitchell has been colorized for this book. The inset map shows present-day state boundaries for comparison.

Britain named it not for the man, but for the river and bay that bore his name.

Delaware's history reminds us of several important themes in America's history. Perhaps most importantly, it highlights how the land now encompassed by state boundaries was the province of many peoples over time. The borders we now recognize as defining the state of Delaware, from the Atlantic Ocean and Delaware Bay on the east, to the sharp, straight-line boundaries that separate it from Maryland on the west and south mark a territory within the United States of America that was hard won. That same land was once part of some much larger and much differently shaped natural and political territories.

A 1750 carving of a mythical creature probably representing the Great Horned Serpent, a spirit believed by the Lenni-Lenape to be evil.

Long the home of Native Americans, including the Lenni-Lenape, Delaware was part of lands on what we call the Delmarva Peninsula (because it includes parts of Delaware, Maryland, and Virginia) and a larger system of waterways (including the Delaware River). This region was claimed by several European empires and other English colonies before it officially became part of Pennsylvania in 1682, gained some independence from Pennsylvania in 1704, and eventually declared itself independent of both Pennsylvania and Great Britain during the Revolutionary War. Then it became the state of Delaware that is familiar to us not only as the "first state," so-called because it was the first of the American states to ratify the Constitution, but also as the second smallest state.

Why did so many different groups of people want to claim this land? Delaware may be small, but it has an attractive geography. Native people could appreciate the rich fishing and farming made possible by the ocean, the bay, and the river as well as the many smaller streams. Europeans liked the cozy position of the bay, tucked away from but still accessible to the ocean traffic of the Atlantic. Eventually the proximity to other centers of population and commerce, including Baltimore, Philadelphia, and New York, made good markets for Delaware's own growing manufactures and agriculture.

Delaware is a small state, but it offers us a lot of interesting historical questions to consider. For example, how can we understand the history of a place before it has its current borders? It can be difficult to fully understand the outcome of a struggle over who would live on the land and who would govern if we don't have many accounts from some of the key groups—especially Native Americans—in that struggle. *Voices from Colonial America: Delaware,* by examining the past from a variety of points of view, provides an excellent means for exploring the people and events that shaped the colony.

First Encounters

THE DUTCH CLAIM LAND *in the New World along Delaware Bay. Swedish settlers establish a short-lived colony and meet the Lenni-Lenape and Nanticoke peoples.*

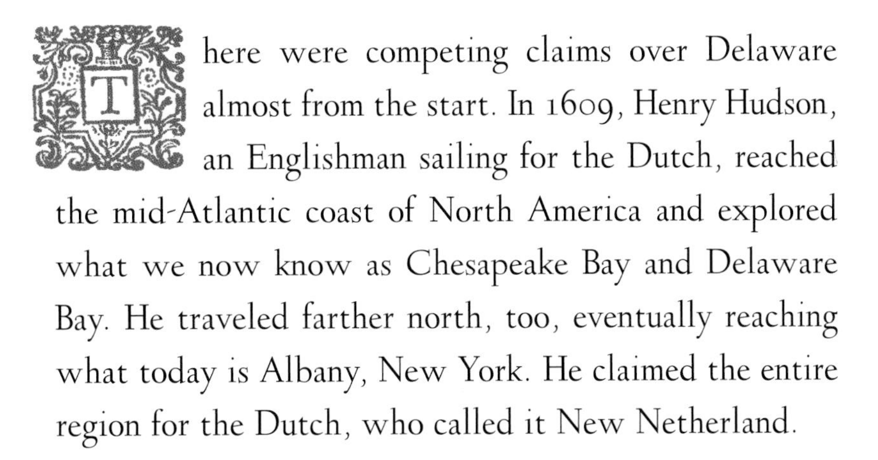

There were competing claims over Delaware almost from the start. In 1609, Henry Hudson, an Englishman sailing for the Dutch, reached the mid-Atlantic coast of North America and explored what we now know as Chesapeake Bay and Delaware Bay. He traveled farther north, too, eventually reaching what today is Albany, New York. He claimed the entire region for the Dutch, who called it New Netherland.

OPPOSITE: A representation of a Susquehanna village along the Susquehanna River shows a palisade surrounding the cluster of domed structures that served as shelter for different families in a clan. Some Susquehanna are gathered around a fire, perhaps for a ceremony; others work outside the palisade in a garden.

In 1610, British explorer Samuel Argall set out from Virginia and investigated lands farther north. He came upon a bay that he named after the man who was governor of Virginia at the time, Lord De La Warr. The Dutch did not acknowledge the British name, however, and called the bay South Bay and the river that flowed into it the South River.

European rulers saw the New World as a place of huge promise. The Spanish had reaped great treasures in gold and silver from the native people of Mexico and South America. They and other European powers hoped to find similar riches farther north in what is now the United States and Canada. By the early 1600s, the Dutch were fast becoming the dominant economic power in western Europe. They knew that the French were gaining wealth from furs traded with Native Americans living around the Great Lakes and along the waterways of the St. Lawrence River valley. The Dutch also knew that the English had established Jamestown in the Virginia Colony to the south. The Dutch wanted to take part in this great global expansion and the riches it seemed to promise. Establishing colonies in the area of current Delaware was part of these larger ambitions.

Like the Spanish, the French, and the English, the Dutch would have to deal with the native peoples of the land they hoped to colonize. While the Spanish had a reputation for treating Indians cruelly, enslaving them to extract the precious metals that they prized, the French had to encourage a trading relationship to get the furs they wanted. Following this example, the Dutch negotiated relationships with both the Iroquois in the Upper Hudson Valley and the Algonquian-speaking people in the south. As more and more Dutch arrived, their need for land for farming increased. This led to more conflict with the Indians.

The Delaware

Two Indian nations with strong tribal affiliations lived in the region: the Lenni-Lenape along the Delaware River and the Nanticoke, whose lives centered on Chesapeake Bay. There were also much smaller clans of Indians who banded together and who, over time, would be forced to align themselves with larger tribes for protection against both Europeans and other Native Americans who sought to control the fur trade. (The Lenni-Lenape, Nanticoke, and smaller tribes in the mid-Atlantic region all came to be known as the Delaware, so named by Europeans who encountered them along the Delaware River and in the valleys around it.) Many of these smaller groups had once been part of larger tribes. In the early 1600s, as European colonization was under way, many Indians were infected with diseases such as smallpox, against which they had little resistance. A large group of Iroquoian

smallpox—a disease caused by a virus that leaves blister-like sores on the skin

Susquehanna, also called the Minqua, would eventually absorb some of these smaller clans, creating shifting alliances that would one day affect European settlement and the Indians' survival.

The Lenni-Lenape lived along the mid-Atlantic seaboard of North America, fishing the abundant waters of the Delaware River and Bay in hollowed-out canoes. This engraving appears in a pamphlet titled "A S[h]ort Description of the Province of New Sweden, now called by the English, Pennsylvania in America."

The Lenni-Lenape

The Lenni-Lenape, or "true people," lived in great numbers along the mid-Atlantic seaboard on lands that now form the states of Delaware, New Jersey, New York, and Pennsylvania. The Lenape were mainly farmers, planting crops among the small villages they lived in along the Delaware River and the streams feeding it. The Indians lived in domed structures covered in bark and grass.

Unlike the Iroquois to their north, the Lenape were not organized into a strong confederacy. The tribe migrated to new regions with the seasons in order to farm land and take advantage of plentiful hunting grounds. The smaller clans formed alliances and made agreements within their own society regarding hunting grounds, fishing areas, and plots for planting. The Lenape, like all Native Americans, had no understanding of "owning" land. A region belonged to the clan or tribe who inhabited it for a certain period of time or until the land was exhausted and the group moved on to a new settlement.

The Nanticoke

Once a large tribe roaming parts of what are now Maryland and Delaware, the Nanticoke lived along the eastern banks of Chesapeake Bay. The word "Nanticoke" means "tidewater people." Excellent hunters and fishermen, the Nanticoke were well respected by the neighboring Lenni-Lenape in the north. Although similar in culture to the Lenni-Lenape, whom they considered their relatives, the Nanticoke spoke their own version of the Algonquian language. The Nanticoke were also experienced beadmakers, and their valuable wampum made them attractive trading partners to other tribes in the region, as well as to the Europeans who would come to inhabit their land.

wampum—small beads made from polished shells that Native Americans used as money

The Nanticoke were skillful farmers. Their villages were often surrounded by log fences, protecting them from raids by enemy tribes.

It has been recorded that the first contact between the Nanticoke and the Europeans occurred when Captain John Smith led an expedition up Chesapeake Bay from the English colony at Jamestown in 1608. Unfriendly at first, the Indians eventually communicated with Smith and let him pass through their territory. Smith recorded that about 200 warriors lived around the bay, many of them with wives and children. During the next 30 years, however, as the Maryland Colony was established in the region of the Chesapeake, the Nanticoke's numbers decreased. Their farmland and hunting grounds were taken over by English settlers. The Nanticoke were eventually forced to align themselves with the Lenape, and later the Iroquois.

Because of the shifting alliances within their own clans, diplomacy was second nature to these tribes. In many ways, their familiarity with treaties benefited the Europeans upon their arrival in the New World. The newcomers encountered native peoples who were willing to share the bounty of the land so everyone could prosper. Native Americans soon realized, however, that Europeans had different views of land ownership. The Indians did not agree with the European system of selling land outright and losing all access or claims to that land for the future. In addition, as tribes were wiped out by European diseases, tensions developed. The formerly positive relationships between settlers and Indians declined.

Once they obtained land from the Indians and instruction in planting and hunting the area, the Dutch settlers had little use for the natives who did not provide them with furs to trade. The Lenape, who believed they had the right to live and hunt on the land they had sold to the Dutch, were soon expected to pay taxes to the colonists in the form of bounty from their crops, furs, or wampum. Of course, the Indians refused to pay this tax and were soon forced to rethink their negotiations with each other and with the white settlers.

In this 17th-century print, Dutch settlers fire at Indians who are shooting arrows to keep them from coming ashore. Violence between the Dutch and Native Americans erupted throughout the mid-1600s.

These shifts led to violence. In 1643, war between the Lenape and the Dutch broke out. The Indians succeeded in driving the Dutch as far as Manhattan. Although a peace agreement was reached, violence spread again in 1655, and many Dutch settlers were killed at the hands of the Lenape. Eventually, the Indian population dwindled from warfare, disease, and alcoholism to the point that they could not defend themselves. By the end of the 17th century, only small numbers of Lenape and Nanticoke were living along Delaware and Chesapeake Bays, coexisting with the English colonists.

In the years ahead, as Sweden sought to gain a foothold in the New World, the Lenape and Nanticoke migrated to what is now Pennsylvania where the Quaker William Penn, founder of the colony, would treat them with kindness and respect.

The Dutch in the New World

The Dutch West India Company set up operations in New Netherland in 1624. It hoped to rival the success of the Dutch East India Company, founded in 1602, that had sent ships all over Asia in pursuit of the silk and spice trades. The government hoped the Dutch West India Company would help make the Netherlands the most powerful nation in Europe. The company was charged with the responsibility of settling in the New World and finding natural resources there.

This 1694 print shows the Dutch East India Company shipyard in the Netherlands, with ships docked in the harbor, warehouses to hold goods for import and export, and a large boat being built.

The Dutch West India Company set up operations in New Netherland in 1624. It intended to start a whaling and fishing colony on the land on either side of South, or Delaware, Bay. The area was attractive because of its important location—the country that took control of this area could control shipping up and down the Delaware River. The river flowed northward into what is now New York and southward to Delaware Bay and, ultimately, into the Atlantic Ocean, so fishing and whaling ships could sail to the ocean, then return to the safety of the bay. In 1631 the company bought a 16-square-mile (41-sq-km) piece of land from Lenni-Lenape chiefs. The tract of land extended from Cape Henlopen, near present-day Lewes, Delaware, northward to the mouth of the South (Delaware) River.

Peter Heyes, captain of a Dutch ship called the *Walrus*, brought the first European settlers to Delaware. They sailed from the Netherlands in 1631. When the settlers arrived, they saw many swans gliding on the surface of the river, so they called their new settlement Zwaanendael, which means "Valley of the Swans." At Zwaanendael, one mile (1.6 km) from present-day Lewes, near the mouth of Lewes Creek, the settlers built a fort they called Oplandt and surrounded it with a palisade. When the fort was complete, Captain Heyes put Giles Hossett, a ship's officer, in charge and sailed the *Walrus* back to the Netherlands.

palisade—a fence made of sharp sticks used for defense

Massacre

In 1632, David Pieterson De Vries, an investor in the West India Company, sailed from the Netherlands with more immigrants to join the settlers at Zwaanendael. Even before they set sail, however, the voyagers heard rumors that the settlement had been destroyed and all the settlers killed. De Vries wrote in his diary, "*We understood that our little fort had been destroyed by the Indians, the people killed two and thirty men who were outside working the land.*" The shipload of anxious settlers soon discovered that the rumors were true. On arriving, De Vries wrote that all that was left of the settlement was *"skulls and bones of our people and the heads of horses and cows which they had brought with them."*

A portrait of David Pieterson De Vries

Historians are unsure about what truly happened at Zwaanendael. DeVries published an account of his investigation of the massacre in his book *Voyages*. According to an Indian from a nearby village who discussed the incident with him, the Dutch settlers had fastened a sheet of tin painted with the coat of arms of the Netherlands onto a column. One of the Indian chiefs thought he could use the tin to make a good pipe for smoking tobacco, so he removed it. The Dutch settlers thought that the chief's act showed disrespect to the Netherlands. De Vries understood from what the Indian told him that

coat of arms—a symbol of a country, tribe, family, or other group

> *those in command at the house made such an ado about it that the Indians, not knowing how it was, went away and slew the chief who had done it, and brought a token of the dead [chief] to the house to those in command, who told them that they [the Dutch] wished that they [the Indians] had not done it; that*

> *they should have brought him to them, as they [the Dutch] wished to have forbidden him not to do the like again.*

The Indians believed that they were acting honorably by killing the chief and that the Dutch would forgive them for the chief's actions. But the Dutch, who had only wanted to warn the chief not to do something like that again, were dismayed to learn that the Indians had taken their leader's life.

De Vries was told that the friends of the murdered chief planned their revenge on the Dutch:

> *Observing our people [the Dutch] out of the house, each one at his work, that there was not more than one inside, who was lying sick, and a large mastiff [dog], who was chained . . . and the man who had command standing near the house, three of the stoutest Indians, who were to do the deed, bringing a lot of bear-skins with them to exchange, sought to enter the house. The man in charge went in with them to make the barter, which being done, he went to the loft where the stores lay, and in descending the stairs one of the Indians seized an axe and cleft his head so that he fell down dead.*

The Indians then killed the rest of the inhabitants of the fort and burned it to the ground.

De Vries realized that his newly arrived settlers would not succeed without a peace treaty with the Indians. Though a truce was soon agreed upon, most of the colonists decided to return to Europe. The colonists were inexperienced at whaling, the work for which the settlement was intended, and had found little success. DeVries and the settlers sailed for the Netherlands on April 14, 1633.

New Sweden

In 1637, the Swedish government formed the New Sweden Company with the goal of setting up a colony along the banks of the Delaware River. At the time, Sweden included Finland as well as parts of present-day Russia, Poland, and Germany. The New Sweden Company included Swedish, Dutch, and German investors who were interested in making a profit by trading for furs and tobacco. Both these products were highly prized in Sweden and throughout Europe, and the new company hoped to bypass the British and French merchants who sold these goods. Tobacco was already being successfully grown in the English colony of Virginia, and fur trapping and trading were a thriving business in the region. The Swedes planned to send the goods to Europe, where they would be sold. Like the Dutch before them, the Swedes hoped that profits made from this colony would help expand their influence and power in Europe.

In the early months of 1638, a Dutchman, Peter Minuit, guided the *Kalmar Nyckel* and the *Fogel Grip*, up the South (Delaware) River. Minuit was determined to meet with the Lenni-Lenape chiefs to negotiate the purchase of land on the west bank between the Delaware River and the river that the Swedes later named Christina, after

Sweden's young queen. New Sweden's colonists immediately set to work building Fort Christina, which faced the Christina River on a site they called The Rocks. Minuit must have believed he had purchased permanent title to the land for his colony. The Lenape, however, based on their culture, would have intended the deal to be only temporary and subject to change.

Swedish settlers come ashore on Delaware Bay to explore the rich and bountiful land. The settlers named this spot Paradise Point and continued up the river to where they would build Fort Christina.

The Swedish government needed more people to settle in the colony, so it ordered that married soldiers "*who had either evaded service or committed some such offence*"—in other words, deserters or soldiers who had committed minor crimes—be sent to the colony as punishment for their offense. The soldiers' families were allowed to go, too.

Finns living in Sweden were another target. Some of them resisted conforming to Sweden's religion and paying the high taxes the government demanded. The government knew that these Finns looked for work in mines and lived free of charge in the forests, where they burned trees to clear land to grow crops. For these reasons, the Swedish government pushed local governments to persuade the Finns to sail to New Sweden. Some of these colonists were even criminals who were given the choice of being put to death for their crimes or sailing to the New World. When the settlers already established at the colony realized that many of the new colonists were criminals, the colony sent them back to Sweden. According to one who returned, New Sweden had passed a law that kept Swedish and Finnish criminals out of New Sweden because the colonists feared that God would not bless their colony if it were inhabited by criminals. "*It was after this forbidden, under a penalty, to send any more criminals to America. Lest Almighty God should let his vengeance fall on the ships and goods, and the virtuous people that were on board,*" he said.

Governor Printz

During its first years, the colony of New Sweden did not make a lot of money for the New Sweden Company. One reason was that the colonists could not compete with Dutch

ORNAMENTS *for the* Indians

THE DELAWARE INDIANS PRIZED the endless supply of fascinating trinkets the Europeans brought to America. Until the Europeans landed in North America, the Native Americans had probably never seen a mirror or a gilded chain, and they were eager to receive these items in trade with the new settlers. Indians used these items to ornament their clothing or as part of ceremonies. They often used European goods in creative ways into their culture, giving Indian meaning to European things.

According to historical records, the *Kalmar Nyckel* carried in its hold "*dozens of tobacco pipes, mirrors and looking-glasses, gilded chains and finger-rings, combs, ear-rings and other ornaments for the Indians,*" along with hunting and farming supplies for use by the settlers.

and English merchants who traveled through the region and had already established trading relations with the Indians. These merchants had large stores of goods, including mirrors, knives, and brass pots to trade for furs.

The Swedish government took over the colony's leadership in 1642. Johan Printz was named as the new governor of the colony. The colonists needed items to use as barter with the Indians, so Printz requested more trade goods from the Swedish government. After several months, the items arrived and the colonists began to trade more actively with the Indians. They soon discovered that the local Lenni-Lenape spent most of their days fishing and farming, not trapping furs, so the settlers traveled farther inland to Minqua territory to find Indians who could increase the supply of pelts.

Printz also found out that the settlers depended on the Lenape for some of their food, such as maize. A letter he wrote to the Swedish government shows that the Swedes wanted to take more land from the Indians. Printz requested the government

maize—a type of corn grown by Native Americans and early American colonists

to send over here a couple of hundred [colonists] . . . until we broke the necks of all of them [the Lenape] in this River, especially since we have no beaver trade whatsoever with them but only the maize trade. They are a lot of poor rogues. Then each one [colonists] could be secure here at his work and feed and nourish himself unmolested without their maize, and also we could take possession of the places (which are most fruitful) that the savages now possess.

While waiting for more settlers to arrive, the colonists built a brewery and a wharf. They also planted tobacco. As New Sweden began to prosper, most settlers had high hopes for its future. Indeed, the settlement lasted for almost 20 years, until the Dutch reasserted their claim to the area and Printz returned to Sweden.

wharf—a structure built along a shoreline where ships receive and discharge passengers and goods

CHAPTER TWO

The Swedish and Dutch Compete

THE DUTCH TAKE OVER the Swedish settlements for just a short while before the English arrive to secure control of the region and make it part of New York Colony.

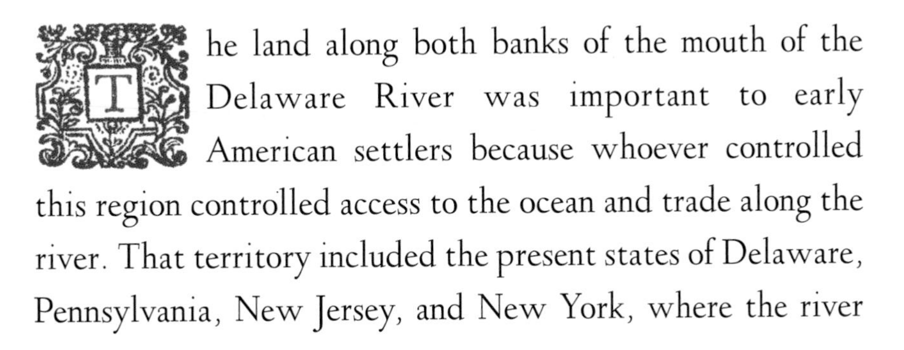

The land along both banks of the mouth of the Delaware River was important to early American settlers because whoever controlled this region controlled access to the ocean and trade along the river. That territory included the present states of Delaware, Pennsylvania, New Jersey, and New York, where the river

OPPOSITE: Peter Stuyvesant (with wooden leg) of New Netherland orders the Swedes at Fort Kasimier (renamed Fort Trinity by the Swedish) to surrender to him on September 11, 1655. A trumpeter and other members of the Dutch party expect an easy victory.

ends. With the establishment of New Sweden on the banks of the lower Delaware, the Swedes maintained that control. The Netherlands, envying the Swedish holdings, instructed the leaders of New Netherland to try to conquer New Sweden and reassert Dutch claims to that area.

In May 1651 the Dutch sent a heavily armed ship up the Delaware to frighten the Swedish. The ship sailed south from New Amsterdam, the capital of New Netherland, up through Delaware Bay into the river and passed back and forth along the shoreline in plain view of the Swedes. Governor Printz responded by ordering his soldiers to meet the ship with one from New Sweden, loaded with cannon and ammunition. Realizing that the Swedes were prepared to defend their land, the Dutch sailed back to New Amsterdam.

A month later they returned, this time on foot as well as by sea. Eleven Dutch ships sailed up the river in June, while 120 men, led by New Netherland's Director-General, Peter Stuyvesant, approached the settlement on the ground. Printz and his men watched them closely, ready to defend Fort Christina, but again the Dutch withdrew. Their message, however, was clear: Stuyvesant intended to take New Sweden and had the men and weapons to do it.

Fort Kasimier

The Dutch finally found a way into the Delaware region, but not through violence. Instead, they declared

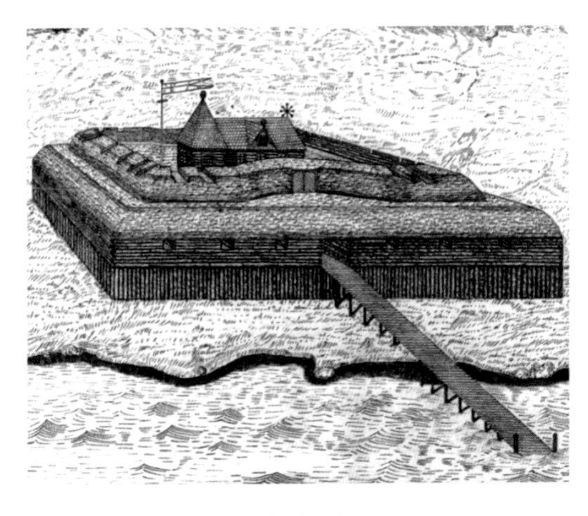

A sketch of Dutch-built Fort Kasimier shows a long bridge leading across the river. The fort was outfitted with cannon and guarded against invaders by two warships.

themselves the rightful owners of not only the land on which New Sweden was settled but also the land to the south of the colony, and they moved in. Stuyvesant claimed that the Dutch had purchased the land from the Minqua, but the Swedes insisted that they had legally purchased the land from the same tribe first and had the official deed to prove it. They sent messengers with the deed to Stuyvesant, but he ignored them. Just below New Sweden's Fort Christina, Stuyvesant built Fort Kasimier. Then the Dutch demanded that all ships sailing upriver to New Sweden stop at Fort Kasimier and pay a duty before continuing their journey.

duty—a tax on imported goods

Alarmed, Printz sent several messages to Sweden asking what he should do about the Dutch action. Three years passed with no word of advice from the Swedish government. Some colonists grew weary of waiting for word from Sweden, so they left the settlement and moved to nearby Maryland. In 1653, Printz resigned as governor. That autumn, he and about 25 colonists sailed from New Sweden back to their homeland.

Johan Rising Arrives

In February 1654, the Swedish government sent another expedition to the colony. Johan Rising, the leader of the voyage, brought 350 immigrants with him. Rising was told to take charge of the colony. In May the Swedish ships sailed up the Delaware, where Rising was angered to see Dutch-occupied Fort Kasimier. When the soldiers at the fort stopped his ship and demanded a duty, Rising announced that he was New Sweden's new governor and called upon the Dutch to immediately surrender to the Swedish crown, which was the rightful owner of the territory.

Only about 20 Dutch soldiers were at the fort that day, and they did not have enough weapons and ammunition to fight back, so they surrendered. Rising renamed the fort Trinity, because it was captured on Trinity Sunday, a Christian holiday. Filled with pride over his victory, he continued on to New Sweden.

Plans to Improve the Colony

One of the first things Rising did after arriving was to arrange a meeting with the sachem, or leader, of the Lenni-Lenape. At the meeting, the Swedish leaders and the sachem discussed final arrangements for the purchase of more land along the west side of the Delaware River.

Knowing how important it was to maintain peaceful relations with the Lenape, Rising had brought many gifts for them from Sweden. The Lenape accepted the gifts and agreed to a treaty of friendship.

Rising had been instructed by Sweden to make the colony more profitable, and he quickly set the colonists to work building a sawmill and a flour mill and establishing more business, including tobacco trade. In his 1654 report about New Sweden to the Swedish government, Rising wrote that the colony upon his arrival was "*an empty country, disturbed partly by despondency [despair], partly by mutiny and desertion; nevertheless, God be praised, we still prosper.*" He said that he needed more supplies for the upcoming winter, that he would force the colonists to be more disciplined, and that he would restore their faith in the goals of the colony.

The report told of Rising's plans to continue to settle more colonists along the river around Christina "*in order that one might be the more secure against Virginia [an English colony], and besides to carry on trade with them, making a passage . . . by which we could bring the Virginia goods here and store them, and load our ships with them for a return cargo.*" Rising optimistically described many ways that the colony could make money for Sweden, including breweries and trade in timber and furs.

This Swedish soldier in New Sweden wears the blue and yellow colors of his country's flag

Rising also had plans for expanding the colony. He described how he and New Sweden's engineer, Peter Martensson Lindestrom, were planning to build houses farther out from Fort Christina. He hoped that eventually towns and villages would be established along the river. Lindestrom wrote,

> *The Christina River is a deep river, rich in fish: [it] extends far up into the country [and] can be navigated with sloops and other large vessels a considerable distance. On both sides of this river . . . the soil is by nature suitable for all kinds . . . of agriculture and the cultivation of all kinds of rare fruit-bearing trees. Yes [it is] such a fertile country that the pen is too weak to describe, praise and extol it; on account of its fertility it may well be called a land flowing with milk and honey.*

Swedish settlers harvest their wheat crop using a scythe, a hand tool used for cutting the stiff grass. Fort Christina can be seen in the background of this colored engraving of New Sweden in the 1600s.

Rising was convinced that any attempt by the English or Dutch to settle in the New Sweden area would not be successful because Sweden had a rightful claim to the area and could prove it. At the time, the Swedish colony extended as far north as present-day Chester, Pennsylvania, which was then called Upland. Rising also was negotiating with the Minqua for the purchase of land farther south and west, facing Chesapeake Bay along the Elk River.

The Dutch Return

Rising's attention, however, turned from improving the colony to defending it when seven Dutch ships carrying several hundred men sailed up the Delaware River in August 1655. Peter Stuyvesant, the leader of the Dutch colony of New Netherland, was angry when he learned that Rising had forced the surrender of Fort Kasimier, and he intended to take revenge. He anchored the ships near Fort Trinity and sent a message demanding not only that Rising return the fort to the Dutch but also that he surrender the entire colony of New Sweden to the Dutch West India Company.

After retaking Fort Trinity, which they immediately renamed Fort Kasimier, the Dutch soldiers took over Fort Christina on September 15. Official Swedish rule in North America was ended.

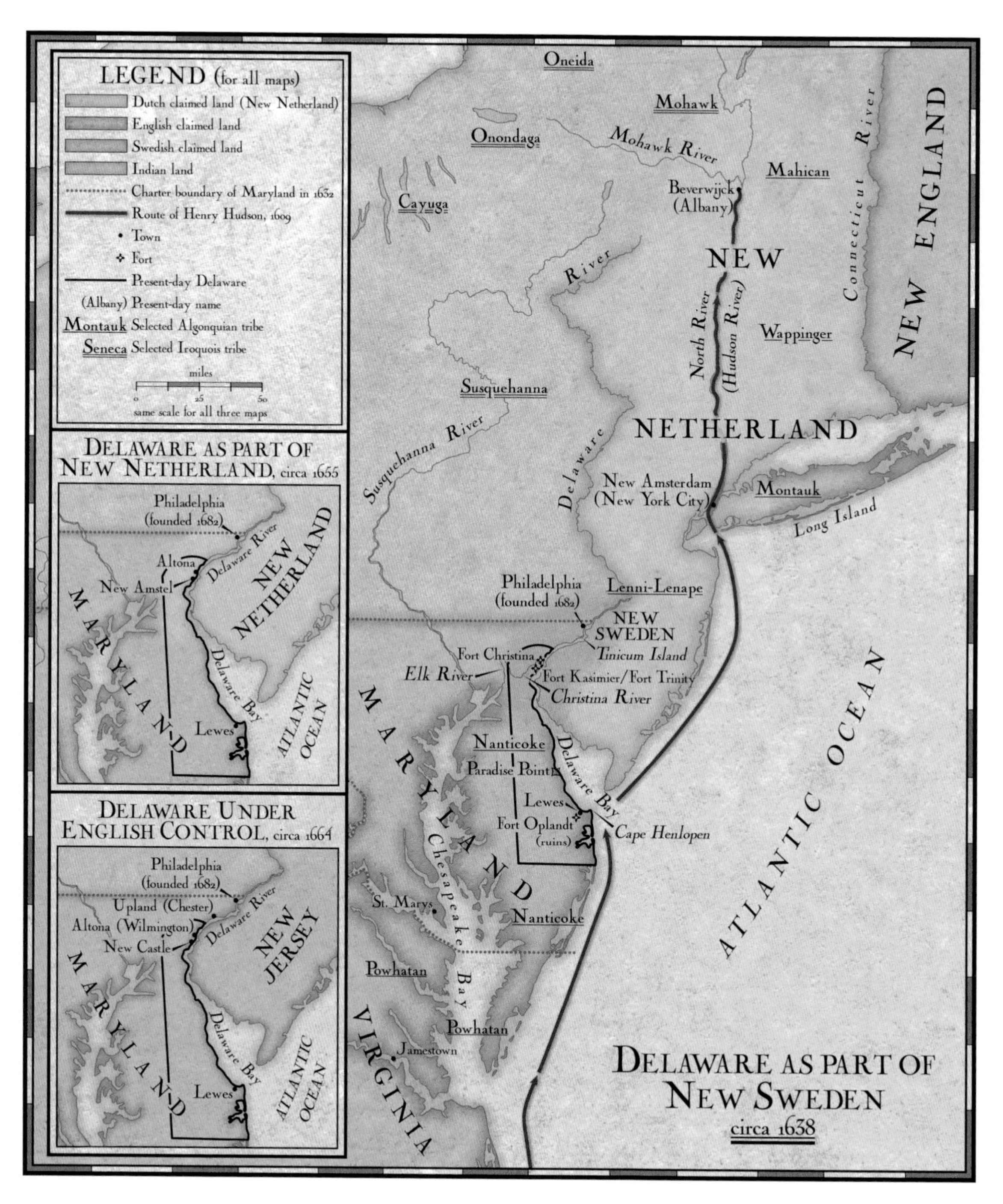

This series of maps shows how the area that would one day become Delaware changed hands over time, being settled first as part of New Sweden, then as part of Dutch New Netherland, and finally coming under English control in 1664. Although the maps show Delaware's present-day boundaries for reference, these were not established until the mid-18th century.

Despite Rising's surrender to the Dutch, the Swedish colonists were allowed to remain and to keep many of their customs and even governmental practices. Swedish settlers with farms were allowed keep them if they wished, although the farmers had to swear allegiance to the Dutch government. The Dutch also allowed the Swedes to have their own government and militia. So many Swedes were pleased with this agreement that only 37 returned to Sweden when given the opportunity.

Life under Dutch rule did not change significantly for the Swedish colonists who remained. In fact, only about one hundred Dutch settlers lived along the banks of the river during the time they controlled the area. The Swedish and Finnish settlers who remained on their lands continued to farm, while the Dutch lived in towns and concerned themselves with trade.

The new Dutch colony was divided into two parts. One was called the Colony of the City and the other the Colony of the Company—the Dutch West India Company. Fort Kasimier was renamed New Amstel and was made the capital of the Colony of the City, and Fort Christina, renamed Altona, became the capital of the Colony of the Company. In a few years, New Amstel had 110 clapboard houses. The colonists drained the local marshland using dikes, as the Dutch did in the Netherlands. The colonists even built a windmill and used its power to grind

dike—a bank of raised earth that holds in water or directs the flow of water

grain. In 1663, the Dutch West India Company transferred ownership of the Colony of the Company to the city of New Amsterdam, so all the Dutch territory in Delaware then fell under the government of that city. Its control, however, would not last long.

The Duke of York's New Colonies

In the mid-1660s, the King of England, Charles II, turned his attention to his holdings in North America. King Charles refused to recognize the claims of the Netherlands to land in North America because he believed that English explorers had long ago claimed those lands for England. Charles also disliked that the English colonies in New England, including Massachusetts, New Hampshire, Rhode Island, and Connecticut, were separated from the English colony of Virginia by a Dutch colony. In March 1664, the King granted land to his

The Duke of York, brother of King Charles II, in an oil painting by Sir Peter Lely

brother James, Duke of York, that included most of what is now New York and New Jersey. Later, he granted James land that included the present-day state of Delaware.

Eager to claim his land, the duke put together a war party of 450 men. Led by Colonel Richard Nicolls, who had been appointed governor of all English colonies on the mainland of North America, they sailed from England in May 1664 with the goal of taking over the Dutch territory of New Netherland. To make sure the newcomers had support in North America, King Charles wrote orders to be delivered to the governors of the English colonies in New England to *"join and assist them vigorously in recovering our right to those places now possessed by the Dutch, and reducing them to an entire obedience and submission of our government."*

commissioner—a government representative sent to handle matters in another country

On September 13, Nicolls instructed English commissioner Sir Robert Carr to take the ships *Guinea*, *William*, and *Nicholas* into the Delaware River and demand surrender of the Dutch territory there. On September 30, the three ships arrived at New Amstel. After three days, the English secured control of the land along the Delaware as far north as the colony of New York, the English name for New Netherland.

CHAPTER THREE

The Lower Counties on the Delaware

WILLIAM PENN ESTABLISHES *the Pennsylvania Colony and receives a grant of more land along the Delaware River. This area becomes the Lower Counties, eventually Delaware.*

hen the English conquered the Dutch colony on the Delaware and made it part of New York Colony, settlers were forced to swear allegiance to the English crown, and Sir Robert Carr changed the name of New Amstel to New Castle. Until English settlers began moving to the colony in about 1676, however, the English occupation had little effect on everyday life there.

OPPOSITE: This engraving shows William Penn being greeted with joy by colonists upon his arrival at New Castle along the Delaware River. Including an Indian in a canoe reflects a popular view of Native Americans.

Some early changes were noticeable, however, within the government of the colony. From 1664 until 1682, the English governed through magistrates who were appointed by the royal governor in New York. The English government now considered the territory around the Delaware Bay part of the larger Colony of New York. Because of the continuing importance of the Dutch people and their leaders, official business was often conducted in the Dutch language. Eventually, though, English magistrates moved in, and meetings were conducted and recorded in English.

magistrate—a person appointed to enforce the law and sometimes to act as a judge

WILLIAM PENN

In 1681, King Charles II agreed to grant William Penn a charter to settle land in America, partially as repayment of political and financial debts the king owed Penn's father. Penn was a leader of the Quakers, a religious sect that believed in a direct, personal relationship with God. Unlike Protestant followers of the Church of England, Quakers did not feel it necessary to participate in the demanding rituals sanctioned by the church. They believed that people needed only to look inside themselves to find spirituality. Quakers were often mocked and persecuted by Puritans, other Protestants (including members of the Church of England), and even the English government.

Penn dreamed of a place where Quakers could live and practice their religion freely. Penn wanted to use the land grant given to him by King Charles to establish a new colony that would be a refuge for Quakers and a place of religious tolerance for all who settled there.

refuge—a place of safety and peace

Penn immediately began making plans to establish the new colony, which he called Pennsylvania. He sent his cousin William Markham to America as his deputy governor in April 1681, and Penn himself arrived in November 1682. He set up the Pennsylvania seat of government in Upland but established a new capital which he named Philadelphia. The charter that gave Penn the Pennsylvania grant made no mention of present-day Delaware, the lands south of Pennsylvania that were owned by the Duke of York.

William Penn, founder of Pennsylvania

Pennsylvania was lush and fertile. The only problem was that it did not have a coastline on the Atlantic, so all ships that sailed to the new colony had to sail up the Delaware River through the Duke of York's lands. The Dutch, Swedish, and English settlers living there posed no problem for the passing ships. But Penn worried that if another country, such as France, gained control of this territory, it would block English access by sea to Pennsylvania. With this concern in mind, Penn asked the Duke of York to grant him more land. The duke agreed to give Penn the territory around the Delaware River. The charter called this new grant the Lower Counties or the Lower Territories. It is this area that eventually became the Delaware colony.

Penn organized an assembly for county leaders at Upland—soon renamed Chester—on December 4. At the Assembly, the Lower Counties were officially united with Pennsylvania, and it was decided that they would share a governor and legislature, or lawmaking body. With this arrangement, present-day Delaware was attached to, but not part of, Pennsylvania. The two areas had to remain separate because they had been given to Penn in two separate charters with separate sets of guidelines.

legislature—a group of elected officials whose job is to make laws

Penn wanted each of his land holdings to seem equal, so he created three counties in Pennsylvania called Philadelphia, Chester, and Bucks. The three Lower Counties that constitute present-day Delaware were New Castle, Kent, and Sussex (*see map p. 57*). The Lower Counties were then divided into hundreds, which were based on an old English method of dividing land. Even today, Delaware is the only state in the nation that calls its county divisions hundreds.

Penn drew up a constitution for the government of Pennsylvania and the Lower Counties that he called the

Frame of Government. Penn's government was representative, and Pennsylvania and the Lower Counties were both given the same number of members in the Assembly. Earlier, Penn had told the justices from the Lower Counties that Delaware would have, fully and equally, the same privileges as Pennsylvania.

justice—a person who administers the law, such as a judge

William Penn (seated), accompanied by other Quakers, argues with Lord Baltimore over the boundary lines between Maryland and Pennsylvania.

Lord Baltimore Opposes Penn

The colony of Maryland was south and west of the Lower Counties, and had been granted in 1634 to the Calvert family, headed by Lord Baltimore. He opposed Penn's claim to the Lower Counties, asserting that he was the rightful owner according to a 1632 land grant from the English crown. The king tried to clear up the disagreement by giving the Duke of York a charter for the Lower Counties, proving that the land that the duke then gave to Penn in 1682 was legally his to give. But before the king could sign it, he was forced to give up his throne in England. As a result, William Penn and the Calvert family continued to disagree for years over who held the rightful claim to the Lower Counties and what would eventually become Delaware.

While at first most people in the Lower Counties were happy with the arrangement that tied them to Pennsylvania, their feelings changed as Pennsylvania grew. The city of Philadelphia, about 35 miles (56 km) north of New Castle, was gaining importance as a port of entry for traders and merchants, and citizens of the Lower Counties feared it would soon overtake New Castle as the primary port in the area. The residents of the Lower Counties also feared that their voice in Pennsylvania's representative government would be overpowered. If they were swallowed up by Pennsylvania, they might not have any say in how they were governed. On the other hand, Pennsylvanians thought it was unfair that the Lower Counties had a smaller population but the same number of representatives in the Assembly as Pennsylvania.

THE MASON-DIXON LINE

IN 1763, SURVEYORS CHARLES MASON AND JEREMIAH DIXON arrived in Philadelphia from England to settle the boundary dispute between the Penns and the Calverts. The Mason-Dixon Line was completed in the summer of 1768.

Surveying was tough work. Mason and Dixon employed a team of men to pull down trees along the path they wanted to mark so precisely. They had to convince Indians to let them do their work. But the most difficult aspect of their task had to do with the measurement itself. Centuries before, sailors and scientists had figured out how to use the stars to measure latitude. But longitude was a much more difficult measure, and the instruments that Mason and Dixon used reflected the best thinking at the time about this problem. Some of the boundary stones marking the Mason-Dixon Line can still be seen.

The surveyors marked an east-west line dividing Maryland to the south, and Pennsylvania to the north, and surveyed the north-south line that divided the Lower Counties of Pennsylvania (now Delaware) to the east from Maryland on the west. They also re-surveyed a 12-mile arc around New Castle and Chester Counties.

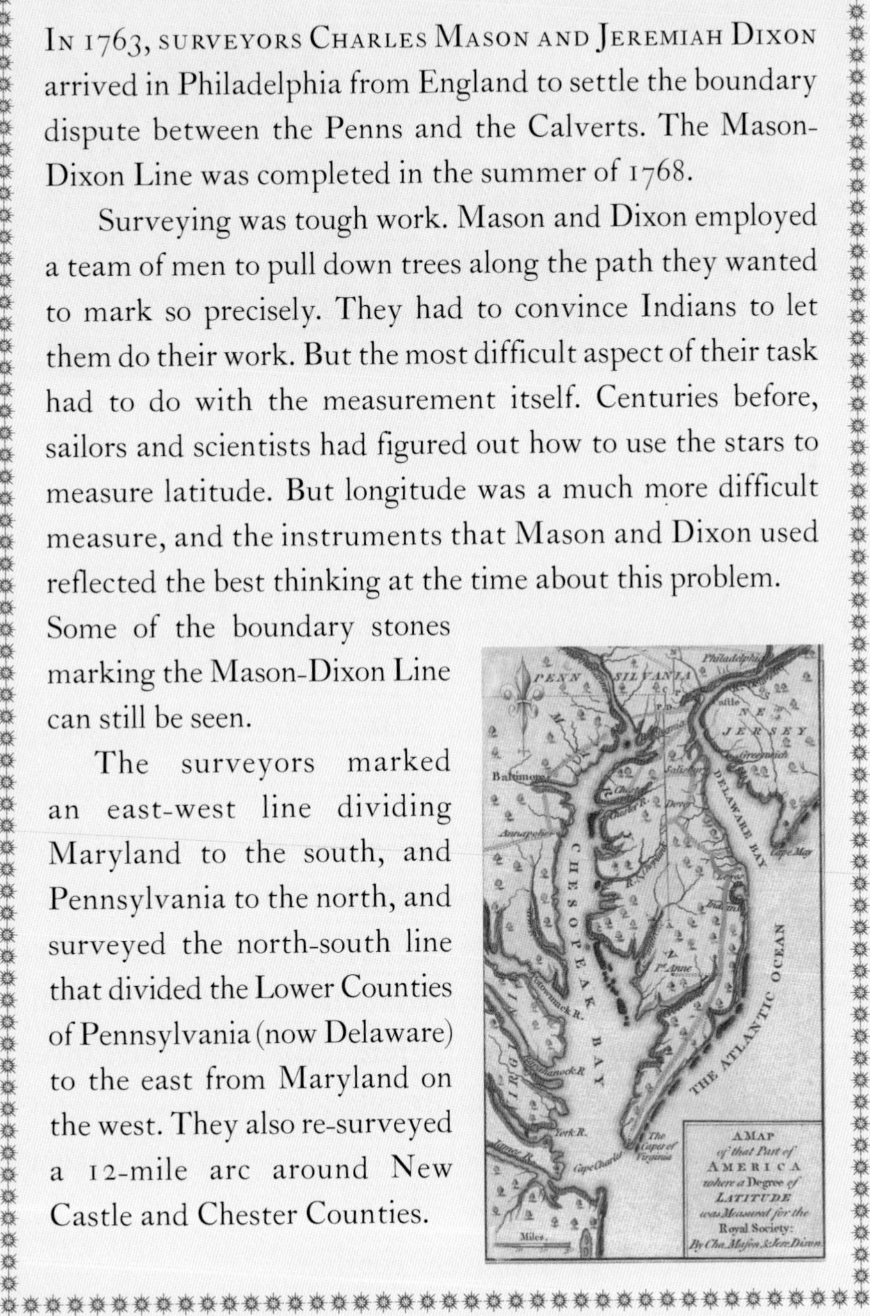

A 19th-century watercolor of 18th-century Quakers traveling to the local meetinghouse for worship in the Lower Counties

Concern About the Quaker Government

The large Quaker population in Pennsylvania also worried Lower County citizens. The Swedish and Dutch people who lived in the Lower Counties practiced religions from their homelands, and English settlers followed the Church of England. Although some Quakers settled in the Lower Counties, most lived in Pennsylvania, where they dominated business and politics. While residents of the Lower Counties were tolerant of all religions, they were concerned about the Quaker belief in peace under any circumstances. Quakers generally refused to fight and always hoped to find a way to prevent conflict.

Conflict always seemed close at hand for the residents of the Lower Counties, however, and they wanted their government to defend them. The settlers who lived along the banks of the Delaware were the first to encounter invaders who sailed in from the Atlantic. At the time, England was at war with France, and French privateers sailed along the American coast, threatening to invade settlements there. The colonists in the Lower Counties lived in fear of such an attack, and they knew that the Quaker government would do little to defend them against the privateers.

privateer—a person or ship licensed or sanctioned by a government to attack enemy ships

Pirates began invading settlements along the Delaware as early as 1685. They soon became more aggressive, attacking Lewes in 1692 and 1698. In 1690 the Lower Counties decided to defend themselves by organizing a volunteer militia, which would fight back if pirates or other invaders attacked again. The Lower Counties hoped that the Quaker government would see the formation of the militia as a cry for help and step aside to make room for leaders who understood the need for defense. When a Quaker from Wales named Thomas Lloyd was appointed president of the Assembly in 1684, the Lower Counties representatives walked out, refusing to attend the legislative sessions. William Penn responded by giving the Lower Counties their own, separate governor, William Markham. Happy that their governor was not a Quaker, the representatives from the Lower Counties returned to the legislature.

In 1684 William Penn left Pennsylvania to return to England. There, he was deeply involved in politics, including the removal of King James II, with whom he had worked closely and well, and the arrival of the new monarchs William and Mary. Penn didn't return to Pennsylvania for nearly 15 years, during which time disputes with the king and queen robbed him of his colonies and put New York's royal governor, Benjamin Fletcher, in charge. The English agreed with the colonists of the Lower Counties that the Quaker government's refusal to defend itself against the French could result in a great loss to England if the French invaded and took over the colony. The French were a growing threat not only because they were moving southward into New England and New York from their Canadian territory but also because they controlled all of Louisiana territory in the south and west.

In 1694, England's King William came to an agreement that allowed Penn to reclaim his colony. But Penn did not return to America until 1699. Throughout the 1690s the disagreement over government continued between the Quakers and the residents of the Lower Counties. In October 1700, in an attempt to reassure the colonists, Penn went to the legislative assembly meeting in New Castle. Several of the Pennsylvania representatives argued that because Pennsylvania had a larger population than the Lower Counties, it should have more representatives in the government. The representatives from the Lower Counties disagreed, because they did not want Pennsylvania to have more power than they did in making laws for their communities. The Pennsylvania representatives also thought that any decisions made in the New Castle Assembly could be declared null and void in Pennsylvania.

This illustration dramatizes William Penn (standing on the platform, wearing a hat) addressing the colonists at the New Castle Assembly.

Under great pressure, in 1704 Penn finally allowed the Lower Counties to have their own legislature, although they would continue to share Pennsylvania's governor. The new, separate assembly first met in November of that year under the Lieutenant Governor of Pennsylvania, John Evans, and with representatives from the three counties of New Castle, Kent, and Sussex. This form of government would continue until 1776, when Delaware became a separate state.

C H A P T E R   F O U R

The Lower Counties Grow

THE LOWER COUNTIES GROW *and prosper. As the Native Americans are pushed out of the region, new borders are drawn.*

The Lower Counties now had their own Assembly, and thanks to a survey completed in 1701, also had the boundary that divided New Castle County from Pennsylvania's Chester County finally marked. Before the work began, surveyors and magistrates from each county met in a conference at William Penn's request. The resulting 12-mile semi-circle is still a distinctive feature of Delaware's boundary.

Penn's health began to fail in 1712, and he died in England in 1718. After Penn's death, he left his land in Pennsylvania to his second wife, Hannah Callowhill Penn,

OPPOSITE: This drawing of a tobacco plantation shows people harvesting tobacco leaves, and a barn with a rack for drying leaves.

and their children. At the time, William Keith was governor of Pennsylvania and the Lower Counties. Keith made many decisions on his own or after consulting with the British government, leaving the Penns out of the process.

In 1724, Keith gave New Castle a new charter that expanded its boundaries and gave it new courts. The Penns were not included in the creation of this charter. Because of Keith's actions, William Penn's widow and her three sons had him removed, and a new governor, Major Patrick Gordon, was named. When Gordon arrived from England, he informed the Penns that the claim to their land in America was once again being challenged. One person who questioned the claim was the Earl of Sutherland, from Scotland, who was owed a great deal of money by the British government. He asked for the Lower Counties as payment. The other person was Lord Baltimore, who based his claim to the Lower Counties on the same conditions he had stated when Penn was first granted the land in 1682.

In an attempt to discuss these claims, the three Penn brothers met with the British King and Lord Baltimore. They agreed to a new border between the Lower Counties and Maryland that gave Maryland a narrow strip of land that once belonged to the counties. After the meeting, the Penns felt sure they had legal claim to the land, but it was not until 1750 that the English court finally determined that they were the rightful owners. This argument eventually led to the border decided and agreed upon by the Mason-Dixon Line.

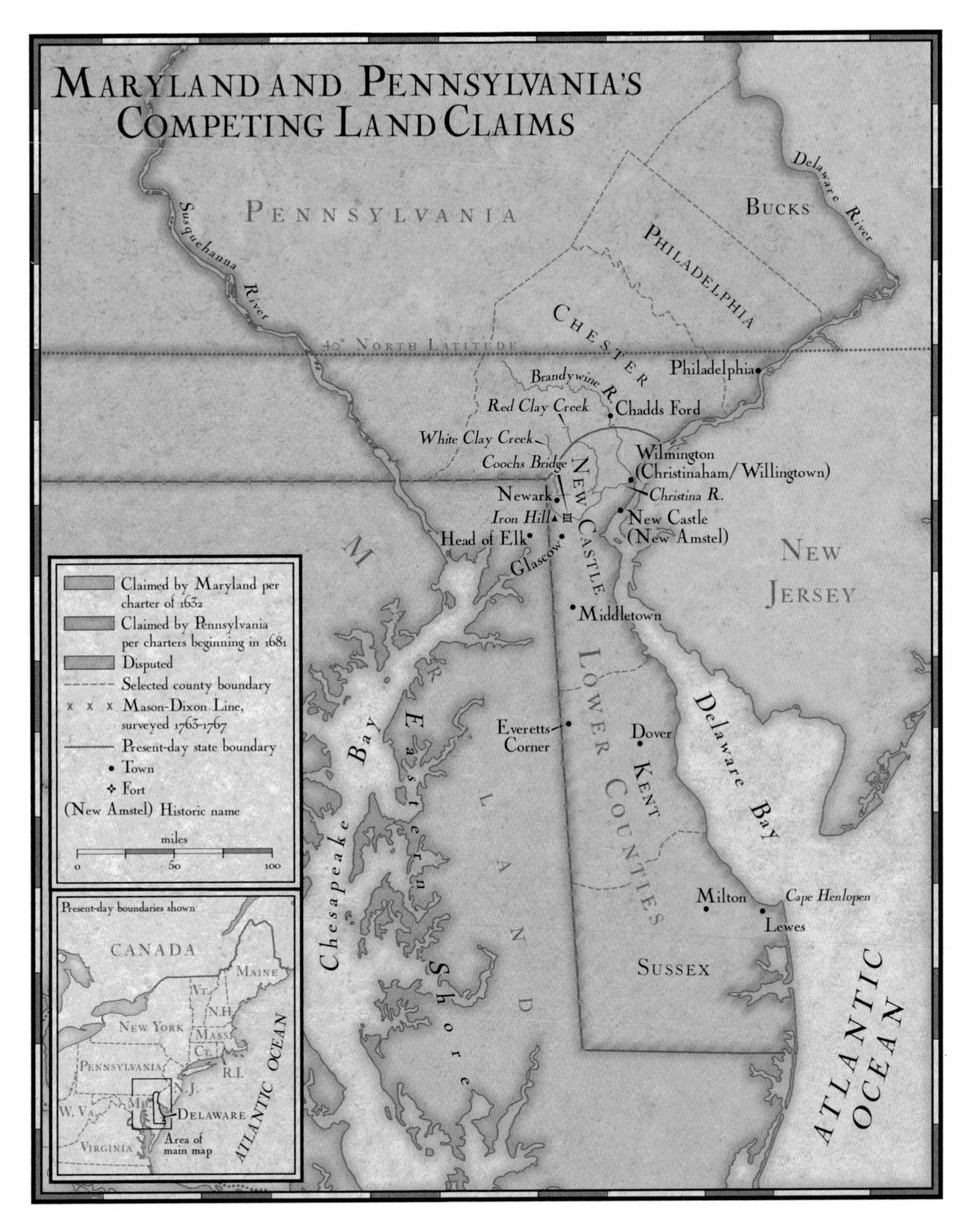

William Penn, to ensure the success of Philadelphia as a commercial center, claimed what he called the Lower Counties (now Delaware) as part of his Pennsylvania Colony in spite of competing claims by Maryland's Lord Baltimore. The boundary dispute was finally settled with the establishment of the Mason-Dixon Line in 1767 (*see page* 49).

The Farming Industry

Overseas trade in and out of Philadelphia still dominated the economy of the Lower Counties. The Lower Counties did not have the trade restrictions that existed in Pennsylvania, so they could sell many goods overseas. The demand for such things as flour and timber strengthened the farming industry. New Castle County was known for its thriving towns, while Kent and Sussex consisted mostly of farm country.

The Brandywine Mills

As it flows from the higher ground of Pennsylvania into the Delaware River, the Brandywine River surges with powerful force, falling 124 feet (38 m) in five miles. In colonial times, its energy was used to rotate the wheels of mills. The wheels were attached to gears that turned grindstones that crushed grain into flour. The flour was then sold to merchant ships in Philadelphia. In 1742 Oliver Canby opened the first large-scale flour mill on the Brandywine for producing flour to be sold overseas. Mills that were built for this purpose were called merchant mills.

By 1764, there were eight mills along the Brandywine. A letter written to the *Delaware Gazette* by a Pennsylvania farmer in 1793 states that by that year there were about 50 mills grinding wheat and corn. In the six months of the mill season, 91,500 barrels of flour were produced.

The earliest mills were built on the less powerful streams that feed into the Brandywine, because at first the rapid water of the river was too much for the colonists to control. Before 1687, the Swedes built a barley mill. Other mills for grinding grain were built during the 1690s. These mostly made flour for local use, not for export. To add more power to the flow of the water, the settlers built small dams made of logs and rocks for the water to rush over.

A mill along the Brandywine River in colonial Delaware is illustrated in this print. By the early 1700s, the Brandywine mills supplied most of British America with paper, including that used in Benjamin Franklin's print shop and the paper on which the Declaration of Independence was written.

Other Industries

Another business that grew out of the mill industry was coopering, or barrelmaking. All the flour that was shipped out of Delaware had to be put into barrels, so there was always a need for more.

Tanneries, where leather was made from animal skin, were built along the Brandywine, Christina, and other Delaware rivers as well. The leather was used to make shoes and boots.

A shipwright (boatbuilder and repairer) hammers wooden nails into the hull of a boat in one of Delaware's many shipyards.

Shipbuilding and timber were other thriving industries in the Lower Counties. Small villages such as Milton, along the Broadkill River, were home to several shipyards. Other shipyards were located in New Castle. Shipbuilders used local timber such as white oak and pine to build ships. Lumber from Delaware was also cut into boards in sawmills along the river and shipped overseas, mostly to England.

The Fate of the Lenni-Lenape

After 1682, the Lenni-Lenape began to move out of the region. The new settlers were taking over their land, and their population was being destroyed by the diseases brought by Europeans, for which they had little resistance.

At first the Lenni-Lenape moved westward, away from the Delaware River. This move resulted in a great shift in their way of life. For generations they had depended on the river for food. Now, as they settled along rivers and streams in the western part of the region, the European colonists built dams that stopped the flow of water, preventing the fish from reaching the western waters. The Lenape went to the Assembly to ask for help in protecting their land. The Assembly promised to help, but nothing was done. In 1757, the native Delaware people began a journey north to an unsettled part of Pennsylvania, leaving behind only a few Indians in present-day Delaware.

Slavery

In the 17th century, the American colonies from the Lower Counties southward raised money by planting and selling crops such as wheat, cotton, and tobacco. Because they wanted to make as much profit as possible from selling their crops, planters turned to slavery. Slaves were not paid for their work—they received only a tiny cabin to live in, food, and one or two changes of clothes a year.

The first African slave in the Delaware area may have been a man called Anthony, brought from the West Indies when the Swedes colonized the region. With the Dutch takeover of New Sweden, slavery expanded in the Lower Counties. The Dutch were making a great deal of money in the slave trade, and they brought Africans to the colony to work on the farms there.

When the English first took over, they had few slaves. But as the tobacco industry grew in the Lower Counties, the colonists, like tobacco growers in Virginia and Maryland, turned to slavery as a labor source. By the end of the 17th century, about 25 percent of the people in the Lower Counties were slaves.

After the Revolutionary War, Delaware banned the slave trade in the state. Slaves could not be brought into the state, although slave owners in Delaware could keep the slaves they had, as well as the children of those slaves. By 1789, slave ships were not even allowed to stop in Delaware ports.

Two Cows and Calves one Colled Bounce the other Dallen	5	10	
Two Cows and yearlings	6	..	
Two Barren Cows	5	..	
one Neagro man Colled Gim	60	..	
one Neagro man Colled Peter	60	..	
one Neagro man Colled Dublen	65	..	
one Neagro Boy Colled Bell	35	..	
one Neagro Boy Colled Spencer	30	..	
one Neagro woman Colled Diner	50	..	
one Neagro Woman Colled Hanner	50	..	
one Neagro woman (old) Colled Hol.	[illegible]	..	
To Fifty Pound of woll	8	15	
Hard Cash in the House	13	19	4
To one Two years old Bull	1	10	
	521	19	4

A 1785 inventory lists slaves and their value as part of Robert Burton's estate at his death. The enslaved people are listed between "Two Barren Cows" and "Fifty Pound of woll [wool]." Burton used slaves to farm his land southwest of Lewes, in Sussex County.

CHANGES IN THE LOWER COUNTIES

The Lower Counties and Pennsylvania became more prosperous as immigration increased. Reverend Israel Acrelius, in his 1759 book *History of New Sweden*, talked about some of them:

> *The times within fifty years are as changed as night is from day. . . . Then many a good and honest man rode upon a piece of bear-skin [in place of a saddle]; now scarcely any saddle is valued unless it has a saddle-cloth with galloon [lace or embroidery] and fringe. Then servants and girls were seen in church barefooted; now young people will be like persons of quality in their dress; servants are seen with perruques de Crains [wigs] and the like; girls with hooped skirts, fin stuff-shoes [shoes made of fabric], and other finery. Then respectable families lived in low log-houses, where the chimney was made of sticks covered with clay; now they erect painted houses of stone and brick in the country. Then they used ale and brandy, now wine and punch. Then they lived upon grits and mush, now upon tea, coffee, and chocolate.*

George Read's home in New Castle, Delaware, was a grand mansion. Today the town boasts many reminders of the time when this signer of the Declaration of the Independence lived.

The nearby city of Philadelphia contributed to the growth and sophistication of the Lower Counties. While Philadelphia remained the largest city in the area, another city, Wilmington, was prospering in the Lower Counties.

IRON HILL

In northwestern Delaware, near Newark, is a hill that rises out of otherwise flat land. It is called Iron Hill, and it played a role in the histories of several groups. The Native Americans of Delaware gathered a kind of stone called jasper there from which they carved arrow points. They called the hill Marettico, which means "hill of hard stone," and Suquaschum, which means "iron." The Minqua built a fort on the hill in the 1660s. The name "Iron Hill" first appeared on a map made in 1672.

In 1701, William Penn set aside 30,000 acres (12,000 ha) in and around the hill for a religious group in Wales, giving them the opportunity to come to America to worship freely. Upon hearing about the iron in the hill, Welsh miners also came to live on the land and mine the iron. Historians searching the hill in later years found an old tunnel dug by the Welsh miners, and in the tunnel they discovered a rusted shovel and an old candle.

Iron Hill was last mined in 1891. Today, mining is no longer allowed there or on nearby Chestnut Hill, which was also found to contain iron ore. The Iron Hill Museum preserves the history of the area, and visitors stroll the hill's trails to see the wildlife.

Founding of Wilmington

In 1728, Thomas Willing married the daughter of an Englishman who owned much of the land in the area where Wilmington is today. In 1731, her father gave Willing a tract of land there, and he designed and began building the village of Willingtown as a port for the grain trade and a marketplace for farmers. He built brick homes and sold them to business people. By 1735 there were 20 houses in Willington, and by the end of 1736 there were 33. That same year, the citizens of Willington asked Governor Thomas Penn for a charter for their village. In 1739 they received their charter and gave the city the new name of Wilmington.

By 1775 Wilmington had a population of 1,229 and was the largest town in Delaware. The total population of Delaware in 1776 was 37,000. In addition to the Swedes, Dutch, Finns, and British who lived there, a new group of immigrants, the Scots-Irish, who started arriving in the 1720s, were settling in Wilmington and nearby New Castle.

While Delaware was growing and prospering, so were other American colonies. Many colonists began to wish that they could be free from British rule. The results of a war between Britain and France would bring great changes that would make the colonists' desire for freedom even stronger.

CHAPTER FIVE

The Road to Independence

Delegates from the Lower Counties attend to the First Continental Congress and begin building a militia to join forces with the Continental Army.

By 1765 there were 13 British colonies in North America, which largely governed themselves. In the Lower Counties, the Assembly that met in New Castle had most of the authority over general local issues, whereas the governor managed the province as a whole, and the King and his ministers governed the Colonies as a whole.

OPPOSITE: Tax collectors are tarred and feathered and paraded through town in a horse-drawn cart in this illustration, showing a protest by Lower Counties residents against the Stamp Act. Opposition to this law was just one step on the road to revolution for American colonists.

The French and Indian War

From 1754 to 1763, Britain had fought a war with France over land claims in North America. The war was fought mainly on American soil, and both the British and the French recruited Native Americans to fight for them. American colonists also fought in the war on Britain's side. The war was called both the French and Indian War and the Seven Years War, and Britain's victory wiped out France's claims to all territory on the mainland of North America.

The cost of fighting the war was great for Britain, and the King looked for a way to pay for it. Parliament, Britain's lawmaking body, decided to tax American colonists to help pay for the war. They thought this tax was fair, because the war had been fought in America to help the colonists keep their land.

The American colonists disagreed. For one thing, colonists had fought and died in the war, and many thought that was payment enough. They also believed that they should not be taxed by Parliament because they had no representation in that legislative body. The colonists coined the phrase "no taxation without representation," and it soon became a slogan to rally support against Britain's actions. Colonists compared their condition to that of slaves and said that because they had no voice in the making of British laws that affected them, they did not have the same rights as British citizens.

THE STAMP ACT

A picture of the embossed (raised design) tax stamp issued by the British government to raise money from its Colonies shows the British crown and a coat of arms. Along the bottom edge, "shilling" represents the amount the stamp cost.

In 1765, Parliament passed a law called the Stamp Act, which placed taxes on everyday items such as newspapers, playing cards, and other things made from paper. The "stamp" was a piece of paper with a raised design. The stamp indicated that the tax on an item had been paid. The colonists called a meeting to discuss the new law. Delegates from 12 of the 13 Colonies attended the Stamp Act Congress in New York City on October 7, 1765. It was the first time that government leaders from different Colonies had joined together against Great Britain.

The conference included three delegates from the Lower Counties and voted to recommend that colonists boycott the taxed goods. At New Castle in February 1766, a grand jury supported the boycott by refusing to proceed unless the court agreed to stop using taxed paper. The next month, a large crowd in Lewes convinced county leaders to stop enforcing the Stamp Act. The stamp agent for Philadelphia and the Lower Counties was forced by citizens to stop collecting the tax.

grand jury—a group of people assigned to listen to facts and evidence in order to determine whether someone accused of a crime should be tried in court

The passage and attempted enforcement of the Stamp Act caused many colonists in the Lower Counties to think about where they stood on the issue. Some remained loyal to the King and were willing to pay the tax. They believed that the British government kept them safe, and they felt an allegiance to the King and to Parliament. Other colonists were beginning to think that the Colonies should be free from British rule and that they would be better off if they governed themselves. While the people of the Lower Counties continued to live together peacefully, the seeds of revolution were beginning to grow.

More Taxes

Only a year after it introduced the Stamp Act, Parliament repealed it. Parliament did this because the protests and violence that the tax was stirring up in some Colonies made enforcing the law nearly impossible. Not long after the Stamp Act was repealed, however, Parliament passed the Townshend Acts, which taxed glass, paint, lead, and tea. Again, under pressure from the colonists, Parliament soon repealed everything but the tea tax. The colonists remained angry. They felt that by keeping the tea tax, Parliament was sending them a message that it had the right to control the Colonies as it pleased.

repeal—to officially recall a law

John Dickinson, a wealthy landowner from Pennsylvania who had grown up in the Lower Counties, expressed his feelings about the British taxes in a series of letters published in November 1767 in the weekly *Pennsylvania Chronicle and Universal Advertiser*. In one letter, he described how Great Britain was taxing items that the Colonies could not legally purchase anywhere but from Britain:

> *These colonies require many things for their use, which the laws of Great Britain prohibit them from getting any where but from her. Such are paper and glass.*
>
> *That we may legally be bound to pay any general duties on these commodities [necessary everyday items], relative to the regulation of trade, is granted; but we being obliged by her laws to take them from Great Britain, any special duties imposed on their exportation to us only, with intention to raise a revenue [money] from us only, are as much taxes upon us, as those imposed by the Stamp Act.*

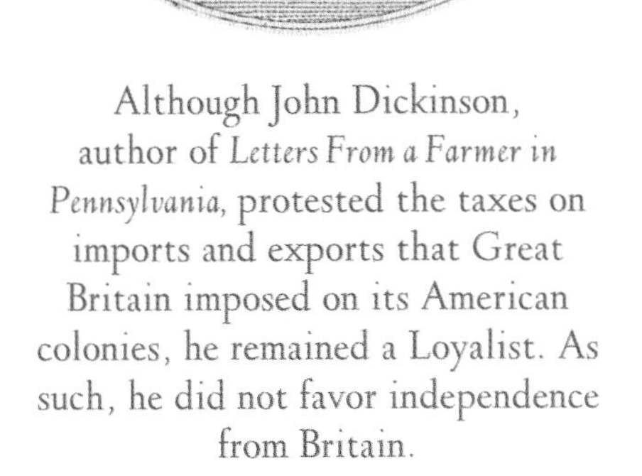

Although John Dickinson, author of *Letters From a Farmer in Pennsylvania*, protested the taxes on imports and exports that Great Britain imposed on its American colonies, he remained a Loyalist. As such, he did not favor independence from Britain.

T. M. Harris, a bystander at the Boston Tea Party, collected spilled tea leaves from the incident and stored them in a glass bottle. This unusual artifact of pre-Revolutionary protest can be seen at the Massachusetts Historical Society in Boston.

THE TEA TAX

While colonists hoped that the King would respond to their protests by lessening Parliament's control over the Colonies, the situation instead became worse. The British sent soldiers to Boston, Massachusetts, where there had been several violent protests against taxation and tax collectors. In 1770, a scuffle on a Boston street ended with British soldiers firing on the crowd, killing five Bostonians.

When news of the "Boston Massacre" spread through the Colonies, they began to protest against British rule even more loudly. Many colonists avoided paying the tea tax by purchasing tea that had been smuggled into the Colonies. The British reacted by imposing the Tea Act, which required that tea from Britain be shipped directly to colonial merchants, who would then have only that tea to sell in their shops. The passage of the Tea Act caused great protests in America. On December 16, 1773, in Boston, a large crowd of men, some dressed like American Indians, descended on ships docked in Boston Harbor. In the ships were wooden crates holding taxed tea. The men boarded the ships and hacked open the crates with hatchets, then dumped the tea overboard. This was the Boston Tea Party. Similarly, in the Lower Counties, protestors helped block a ship with tea on board from proceeding up the Delaware River to Philadelphia.

Angry with the rebellious colonists, Parliament passed the Intolerable Acts. One of these acts closed Boston Harbor to all ships coming in except local ships delivering food and fuel. Another act stated that towns in Massachusetts could not hold meetings without approval from the British government and that the leaders of the colony would be chosen by the British government.

As news of these new laws spread, colonial leaders reacted with concern and sympathy. Samuel Adams of Massachusetts sent a letter to the legislatures of all the other Colonies asking them to form committees of correspondence. Each committee would regularly send letters to the other colonial leaders, informing them what was going on in a particular colony. Adams thought that if the colonists all worked together, they might be able to curb Britain's interference in their governments. Many colonial leaders hoped that they would be able to work out a fair solution to their problems with Britain. Some people, however, were beginning to suggest that it was time for the colonists to gain complete independence from the Crown. In the Lower Counties, meetings were held where the British actions were discussed and condemned. The colonists voted to send help to the people of Massachusetts, who were losing money because few goods could come into the port at Boston. The Assembly named a committee of correspondence with five members: Thomas Robinson, Caesar Rodney, Thomas McKean, George Read, and John McKinly.

Delegates en route to the First Continental Congress in Philadelphia wave to fellow colonists.

The First Continental Congress

On September 5, 1774, delegates from 12 of the 13 Colonies met at the First Continental Congress in Philadelphia to discuss how to proceed with a unified voice in their dealings with Britain. The Lower Counties sent Caesar Rodney, Thomas McKean, and George Read to the Congress. Most delegates felt that the Colonies were not ready to declare total independence from Great Britain. Instead, they hoped to work out with Britain a more satisfactory plan of government and lawmaking.

The situation, however, did not improve. In April 1775, British and American soldiers fired shots at each other in Massachusetts in the towns of Lexington and Concord. Seventy-three British and 49 American soldiers were killed. War now seemed unavoidable. The Lower Counties began organizing a militia for defense and soon had a 5,000-member force. A new army, named the Continental Army, was formed from the troops who were gathering in Massachusetts. The Lower Counties militia trained to be ready to join them. ⁂

CHAPTER SIX

Delaware State

THE LOWER COUNTIES *vote for independence from British rule and adopt a new state constitution.*

In May 1775 delegates attended the meeting of the Second Continental Congress, which would serve as the government of the united colonies during the war. They named George Washington to be the commander of the Continental Army and agreed that all the American colonies needed to join in the war. They voted to approve $2 million to pay for supplies and weapons.

In May 1776 the Continental Congress suggested that each colony form its own government, free from British

OPPOSITE: The Delaware Regiment of the Continental Army marches out of Dover while residents of the newly proclaimed Delaware state gather to watch in this painting titled "Troops Leaving Dover Green."

control. At the Congress, Virginia delegate Richard Henry Lee proposed a resolution declaring that *"these United Colonies are, and of right ought to be, free and independent states."* Because Lee's proposal was so controversial, the Congress decided to hold off voting on the resolution until July 1. That would give time for the delegates to meet with their colonial assemblies to discuss the issue.

resolution—a formal statement voted on by a group as expressing its position on an issue

The Confederation Committee

In June, the Congress named a committee to plan a confederation. For most of their existence, the Colonies had operated nearly independently of each other. Now, they planned to write an agreement showing how they would operate as a more united group while keeping their individuality. Many of them did not want one strong, central government that would have power over all of them. Wanting to keep their own self-rule, they decided that the United States would be a group of separate states that would work in cooperation with one another.

confederation—a group of states or countries that unite for a common goal

The Vote for Independence

In June, the Lower Counties Assembly voted to break off all relations between its government and the British government. The Assembly planned to organize a new government, free from British rule, in the near future. When the Continental Congress met again on July 1, delegates Read and McKean attended, but Rodney was busy at the Lower Counties Assembly. Read thought the call for independence was too hasty, and he planned to vote against it. McKean planned to vote in favor of independence, and he knew that Rodney, if present, would vote for independence as well. McKean, therefore, sent a message to Rodney in Dover that he was needed in Philadelphia. McKean's "yes" vote and Read's "no" vote would cancel each other out, so Rodney's vote was needed to ensure that Delaware voted for independence. As soon as Rodney got the message, he set off for Philadelphia. In a letter dated July 4, 1776, Rodney wrote to his brother Thomas, *"I arrived in Congress (though detained by thunder and rain) [in] time enough to give my voice for independence."*

On July 2, delegates from 12 of the 13 Colonies (New York abstained from voting) voted to pass a resolution declaring themselves free and independent states.

Caesar Rodney

On July 4, the Declaration of Independence, written by Thomas Jefferson, was adopted.

Delaware's New Constitution

On August 27th, the Delaware Constitutional Convention met to begin writing the new document. On September 20, 1776, the new state constitution was adopted.

The new state's system of government consisted of a two-part legislature made up of a seven-member House of Assembly and a nine-member Council. Instead of a governor, the leader of the state would be called the "president and commander in chief." The president would be elected by the legislature, and while the legislature had most of the power in the government, the president did have the power to make a few decisions. For example, he could call up the militia in time of need and call the legislature to special session if necessary. But these decisions would require the approval of a four-member Privy Council before they could be put into action. This council was made up of two members chosen from each branch of the new legislature. These Privy Council members had to give up their legislative seats. With the adoption of the constitution on September 20, 1776, Delaware became the official name of the state.

The constitution also included a section against slave trading. While slaves did work in Delaware's fields, the new government wanted to make it clear that in the future, slaves could no longer be sold in the state. Article 26 in the 1776 Constitution of Delaware states, "*No person hereafter imported into this State from Africa ought to be held in Slavery under any Pretence whatever, and no Negro, Indian or Mulatto Slave, ought to be brought into this State from any port of the World.*" No other state constitution of that time included such a statement. The article did not completely get rid of slavery, but it was a step toward that goal.

The Delaware Militia

By 1775, the Delaware militia already numbered 5,000, and as the war continued more and more men volunteered. A Council of Safety oversaw militia organization and supplies. In the early stage of the war, the Delaware militia was well supplied. As Caesar Rodney wrote on August 8, 1776, to his brother Thomas, "*The Delaware Battalion is under Marching order for Amboy [in New Jersey] Subject to General Washington's further orders. They are Compleatly Armed, as fine Guns as you Could wish to See.*"

battalion—a large military unit

Soldiers in state militias and the Continental Army often carried with them items such as this tin lantern, an open iron lamp on which a lit candle would rest, a wooden plate or bowl with an iron spoon, a clay pipe for smoking tobacco, and a bottle of medicine for minor ailments.

The Delaware militia was made up of five battalions. Three were from New Castle County. Kent County and Sussex had their own battalions. Caesar Rodney was one of the two generals of the Kent County militia. In August 1777, his company stopped the British from raiding Middletown, Delaware, for supplies.

Ratification of the Articles of Confederation

In 1777, the Congress met to review the Articles of Confederation. There was a great deal of debate over several issues.

The issue of states' rights was of great concern to Delaware, which, after Rhode Island, had the smallest population of any state. The Articles of Confederation called for a central legislature, consisting of representatives from all the states in addition to the legislatures of individual states. The number of delegates to this legislature was proposed to be based on a state's population. The main worry of Delaware and other small states was that the larger states would have more representatives and therefore more votes and more power. Thomas McKean of Delaware suggested to Congress that each state should send at least two delegates, but each state would get only one vote. This plan was agreed upon.

Another issue involved the vast areas of land that lay to the west of the 13 states. Some large states, such as Virginia and New York, claimed this land. Delaware and other small states, such as Maryland, feared that these larger states would gain more power in the central government through their ownership of the land. If the large states sold the land for huge amounts of money, they would become much wealthier than other states and therefore, again, more powerful. The small states wanted the large states to turn the land over to the Congress to be used "for the common benefit" of the United States. In 1781, the large states finally did turn over the land to Congress, and soon after Delaware and Maryland ratified the Articles of Confederation.

The Blue Hens

THE NICKNAME OF THE UNIVERSITY of Delaware athletic team, the Blue Hens, comes from the Delaware Regiment, a company of soldiers from the Three Lower Counties formed in 1775. The leader of the Kent County company, Captain Jonathan Caldwell, was a fan of gamecocks, which are roosters that are trained to fight. He carried the roosters with him during the Revolutionary War and often staged bird fights for his troops. The kind of roosters he used were called Kent County Blue Hens. The Blue Hens had a reputation throughout the army for being fierce fighters. Soon, Captain Caldwell's troops also had such a reputation. Other companies started calling them first "Caldwell's Gamecocks" and later "The Blue Hens' Chickens." In 1938, the Delaware General Assembly voted to name the Blue Hen Chicken the state bird.

PROFILE

Thomas McKean

Thomas McKean was one of the most important figures in the development of the state of Delaware. He was born in Pennsylvania in 1734, but spent most of his life in Delaware.

McKean, a major supporter of American independence, was a member of the Continental Congress from its first meeting in 1774 throughout the Revolutionary War. He was named to the committee that drafted the first governing document of the United States, the Articles of Confederation, and he was elected president of Delaware in 1776 and president of the Congress in 1781.

While he was serving Delaware, McKean also held several offices in Pennsylvania, including chief justice of the Supreme Court and governor. He retired from politics in 1812 and died in 1817.

British Troops Move South

In the first years of the Revolutionary War, the fighting took place far from Delaware soil in parts of New York and New Jersey. But then British troops moved southward, determined to capture Philadelphia. In a letter to General Caesar Rodney written on August 31, 1777, George Washington, commander of the Continental Army, wrote,

> *The Congress having called upon the State of Delaware for its proportion of Militia, to assist in defeating the hostile Designs of the Enemy in this quarter,—You are, without loss of time, to use your utmost exertions [efforts] towards accomplishing that necessary purpose, and for assembling and arranging in the best order possible, the quota assigned your State . . . they are to cooperate more immediately with the Militia from the Eastern Shore of Maryland, in watching the motions of the Enemy and taking every opportunity of harassing them, by alarming them frequently with light parties, beating up their Pickets [small groups of troops protecting an army from surprise attack], and intercepting as often as it can be done.*

Only a few days after Washington wrote that letter, British troops entered Delaware on their way to Philadelphia. Their arrival resulted in the only Revolutionary War battle to be fought on Delaware soil. ❋

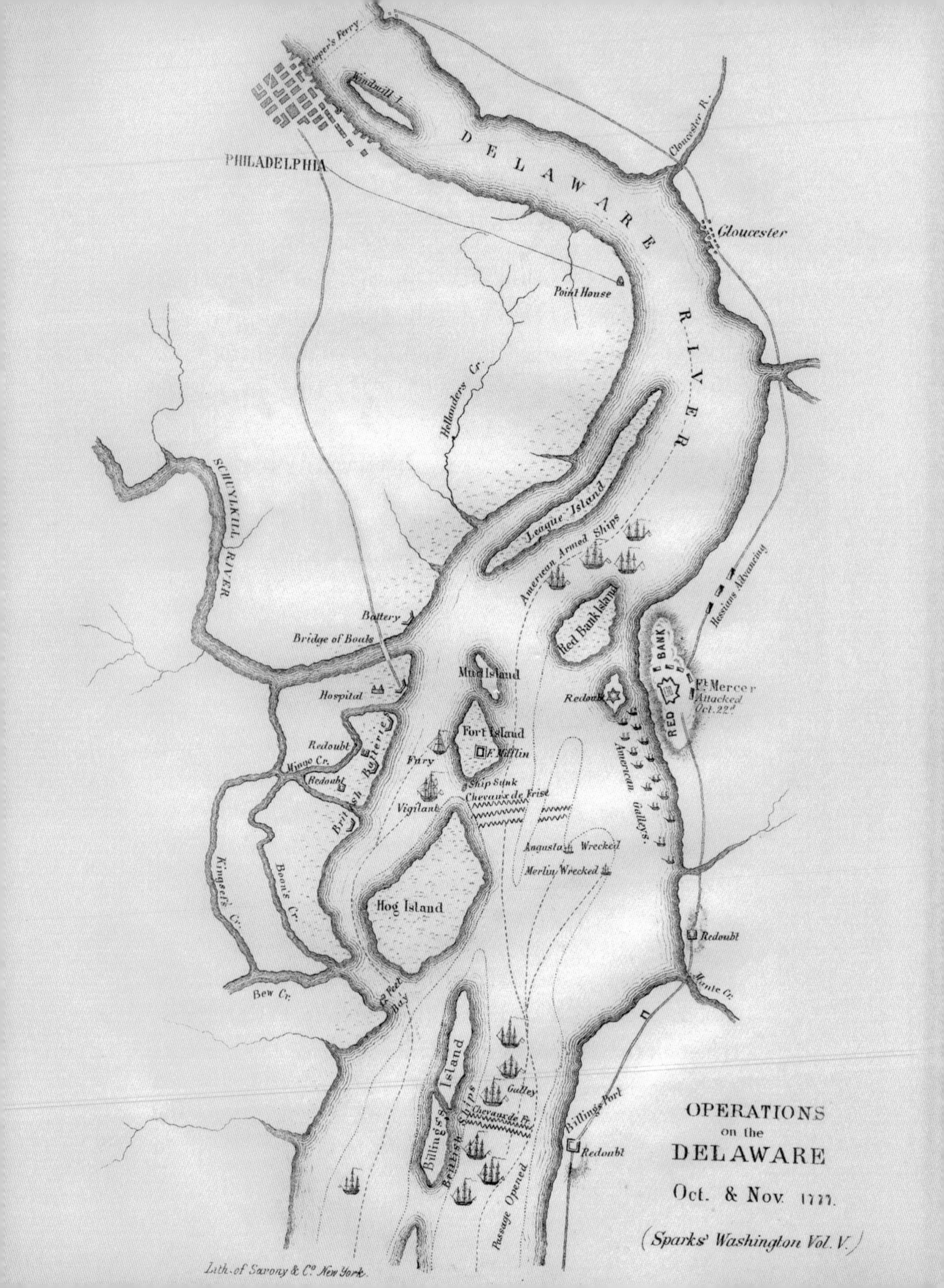
Cooper's Ferry
Windmill I.
PHILADELPHIA
DELAWARE RIVER
Gloucester R.
Gloucester
Point House
Hollanders Cr.
SCHUYLKILL RIVER
League Island
American Armed Ships
Hessians Advancing
Red Bank Island
Battery
Bridge of Boats
Mud Island
Hospital
Redoubt
RED BANK
Ft. Mercer
Attacked
Oct. 22d
Fort Island
F. Mifflin
Redoubt
Mingo Cr.
Redoubt
British Batteries
Fury
Ship Sunk
Chevaux de Frise
Vigilant
American Galleys.
Augusta Wrecked
Merlin Wrecked
Kingsess Cr.
Boons Cr.
Hog Island
Redoubt
Bow Cr.
Ft. Peet
Bay
Mante Cr.
Billings's Island
British Ships
Galley
Chevaux de Fr.
Billings Port
Redoubt
Passage Opened
OPERATIONS
on the
DELAWARE
Oct. & Nov. 1777.
(Sparks' Washington Vol. V.)
Lith. of Sarony & Co. New York.

C H A P T E R   S E V E N

Revolution

BATTLES WITH THE BRITISH *are fought in and around Delaware. Colonists fear for their safety as British ships gain control of Delaware River and Delaware Bay.*

eneral Howe, the commander of the British Army, had two goals for the year 1777. One was to capture the city of Albany, New York, gain control of the Hudson River, and split New England from the rest of the United States. The Continental Army would be prevented from moving south and joining other American troops in their fight against the British. Howe's other goal was to capture Philadelphia. With Albany and Philadelphia under British control, he believed that the Loyalists in America would put pressure on the Patriots to surrender.

OPPOSITE: To get supplies, British troops occupying Philadelphia needed to gain control of the Delaware River. This 1777 map shows the two American forts—Mifflin and Mercer—that defended the river, obstacles (squiggly lines) planted by Patriots, and the locations of British and American ships. The British eventually destroyed the forts and won the river.

The British Move South

General Howe's troops spent the winter in New York. In June 1777, a huge flotilla of 265 British ships sailed south from New Jersey. It looked like the invasion of Philadelphia was about to begin.

On August 25, the flotilla arrived at Head of Elk (today Elkton), Maryland. Howe had to unload 17,000 soldiers, plus weapons and horses, from the ships. General Washington rode to the top of Iron Hill, in Delaware, to watch the British movements. From there, he could see both Chesapeake Bay and the Delaware River. But from such a great distance, it was difficult to tell just how many British troops there were. Washington later wrote to the Congress that from his position, "*I could not find . . . an estimate of it from the distant view I had of their encampment.*" The next day, Washington rode to his Wilmington headquarters, and Howe and his troops made camp just outside of town.

The next morning, the British were on the move again. One man who watched the British troops wrote in his diary that they were "*a beautiful sight to see . . . as they came in sight on the river slope west of the town, with their scarlet coats, their bright guns and bayonets gleaming in the rays of an early August sun.*"

The residents and the outnumbered Delaware militia fled, taking as many supplies as it could find so the British could not have them. The militia members also burned a bridge behind them so the British could not use it.

The British set up camp north of Elkton and began to fan out, looking for food and supplies. On August 30, Washington set up troops at Coochs Bridge, along the Upper Christina River, expecting them to meet up with British troops on the move.

An officer serving with the French Army in America during the Revolutionary War drew this sketch of various soldiers who fought for America.

The Skirmish at Coochs Bridge

Washington's prediction about the British movement was right. On September 2, the main British Army invaded New Castle County, marching to Glasgow. The British troops met up with about 500 American troops on September 3 at Coochs Bridge. While the exact number of soldiers killed was not officially recorded, most historians agree that both sides lost about 30 men.

The Continental Army retreated, but when the British tried to block its retreat and force it to fight, they found themselves cut off from the Americans by Purgatory Swamp. The British could not pass through the swamp, so they went back to Glasgow, where they stayed until September 8. As the British packed up and began to move, the Americans positioned themselves along the east side of Red Clay Creek, prepared to defend Wilmington if the British marched that way. Instead, the British marched northeast into Pennsylvania determined to capture Philadelphia, the capital city of the newly proclaimed United States.

Continental Army soldiers hold their ground against the British at the Battle of Brandywine in 1777 in what would eventually be a victory for the advancing Redcoats.

The British Take Wilmington

British and American troops met near Chadds Ford, Pennsylvania, on September 11 and fought the Battle of Brandywine. The British, who were victorious, quickly moved to occupy Wilmington. They kidnapped Dr. John McKinly, Delaware's president, from his bed in the middle of the night and took important government documents. They kept McKinly as a prisoner of war on two British ships on the Delaware River.

Thomas McKean, who was Speaker of the Assembly at the time, took over for McKinly. He set up a temporary capital at Newark, Delaware, and instructed members of the militia to harass the British in order to drive them out of Wilmington. After five weeks, the British left the city on October 16 and moved on to capture Philadelphia.

The Philadelphia Occupation

In October 1777, the British Army invaded and took over Philadelphia. British troops occupied the city for eight months, until the British government ordered them to move back to New York City. During the occupation of Philadelphia, the British troops were just a few miles from the Delaware border.

Although the British Army had left their state, Delawareans still felt threatened, not only because they were so close to Philadelphia but also because British ships controlled the Delaware River and Delaware Bay. People who lived along the shore worried every day that soldiers would land and plunder their property. They had cause to worry. In 1777 and 1778, British soldiers rowed ashore regularly, looking for food. After the British left Philadelphia in 1778, most of their ships also left the Delaware River and Delaware Bay. One naval ship remained at Cape Henlopen, however, where it guarded the entrance to the bay. Soon after Caesar Rodney became Delaware's president, he wrote a letter to McKean describing the harassment that Patriots endured from the soldiers on the ship and the Loyalists on shore: *"We are Constantly Alarmed in this Place by the Enemy and Refugees, and Seldom a day passes but Some man in this and the Neighbouring Counties is taken off by these Villains . . . many, near the Bay, dare neither Act or Speak least they Should be taken away and their Houses plundered."*

Patriots versus Loyalists

Patriots and Loyalists in Delaware battled throughout the war. The Assembly kept a close watch on them and took over the estates of those Loyalists who were caught helping the British. Thomas McKean wrote, *"The people were dispirited and dispersed; and the Tories [Loyalists], and less virtuous part that remained, were daily employed in supplying the British troops, both in Wilmington and in New Castle, on board the ships of war, with all kinds of provisions."*

This painting shows one artist's interpretation of a confrontation between colonial militia and a Loyalist family. Many Loyalists fled America as it became clear that the British would not easily win the war.

Loyalists also sailed in Delaware Bay, attempting to stop supplies from getting to the Continental Army and looting plantations to get supplies and food for the British. Delaware responded by putting an armed ship in the bay.

In May 1778, President Rodney and his Patriot supporters decided to enforce what they called a test act. This act required anyone who wanted to vote to swear an oath of allegiance to the state government. Some Loyalists responded to the act by leaving the state. Many fled to Philadelphia and evacuated with the British in June.

PROFILE

Cheney Clow

Cheney Clow was a Loyalist who gave Patriots in Kent County trouble. With other Loyalists, he set up a fortification in Gravelly Branch, near present-day Everetts Corner. While historical records are vague about what exactly occurred, it is known that Clow and his followers conducted regular raids on local farms. The farmers finally asked state leaders for help in defending themselves against the Loyalists. In April 1778, Rodney instructed Lieutenant Charles Pope to lead his militia into Kent County. Pope wrote in a report to Rodney, "*I can inform you that the report of the Tories having a fort built is a truth, for this Day myself with a party of about forty, was within a gunshot of their works.*" When Pope's forces approached the fort, the Loyalists fired on them, and they retreated. Pope sent a message to Rodney asking for more ammunition and small cannon. On April 18, he reported that his forces had captured the fort and burned it, but that Clow had escaped. Clow did not return to Delaware until 1782. At that time, the Kent County sheriff's officers went to his homestead to arrest him for treason. Clow responded by shooting at the law officers and killing one of them. He was captured soon after, put on trial, and given a death sentence for the officer's murder. He was hanged in 1788.

THE DELAWARE REGIMENT

Captain Robert Kirkwood of the Delaware Regiment of the Continental Army also had trouble with Loyalists, who continually tried to persuade his soldiers to desert to the British Army. Kirkwood, who fought in 32 battles, wrote in his journal on May 23, 1777, about his dismay at the number of soldiers who deserted to the British side:

> *what is yet more surprising is that there should be persons in the American Army so lost to every principal of virtue, & since [sense] of his own happiness as to attempt desertion to an enemy already destressed [distressed] by famine and worn out fatigue, and who dailey live in fearfull expectation of feeling the weight of American resentment, that this is the situation of the British Army at present all the prisoners and deserters agree. . . . what can induce persons to desert to such a wreched [wretched] enemy.*

The penalty for desertion was harsh. Soldiers were usually punished with 100 lashes on their bare backs and sometimes death. On June 7, 1777, for example, Kirkwood wrote in his journal, "*Francis War and Henery Barrier, both tried by a Genl [General] Court Martial for attempting to desert to the enemy the courts finds them guilty and sentence them to suffer death, his excellence Genl George Washington has approv'd [approved] the sentence the time of execution will be notified in future orders.*"

Soldiers of the Delaware Regiment fought bravely and died in many battles, including those at Long Island, White Plains, Princeton, Trenton, Brandywine, and Camden. Kirkwood's men also fought in South Carolina at the battles of Cowpens and Guilford Courthouse. The total number of soldiers from Delaware to enlist in the Continental Army was 3,763. A Wilmington woman who saw them pass through town described them this way:

> *The shorter men of each company in the front rank, the taller men behind them—some in hunting-shirts, some in uniforms, some in common clothes—come with their hats cocked and some without, and those who did not cock them, not all wearing them the same way, but each man with a green sprig, emblem of hope, in his hat, and each bearing his firelock [gun] with what, even to uninstructed eyes, had the air of skilful training.*

As the war continued, the Patriots in Delaware and elsewhere realized that their fight for independence would be long and difficult. But they pressed on, keeping the goal of freedom in front of them. ❋

DOVER

On May 12, 1777, Dover became the capital of Delaware, probably selected because of its central location in the state. The legislature met in the Kent County Courthouse. In September 1778, Frenchman Louis Philippe Comte de Segur, a colonel in the French Army who had come to help Americans in their fight for independence, described his first view of Dover:

I set out early in the morning for Philadelphia, and I could therefore only see Dover in passing. It was the first American town to which fortune had conducted me. Its appearance struck me; it was surrounded with thick woods because there, as in other parts of the thirteen states, the population was still scattered over an immense territory, a small portion of which was cultivated.

All the houses in Dover offered a simple but elegant appearance. They were built of wood and painted with different colors. This variety in their aspect, the neatness which distinguished them, the bright and polished knockers of the doors, seemed all to announce the order and security, the intelligence and prosperity of the inhabitants.

Pub.by

CHAPTER EIGHT

The First State

THE UNITED STATES *forms a new government, and Delaware becomes the first state to ratify the U.S. Constitution.*

he Revolutionary War continued until British general Charles Cornwallis surrendered to General Washington at Yorktown, Virginia, on October 19, 1781.

The Articles of Confederation had been the frame of government for the United States since they were ratified in 1781. But not everyone was happy with that form of government. The articles did not give the U.S. government the power to impose taxes or raise an army. To pay government debts that resulted from the Revolutionary War, the Congress had to approach each state government and

OPPOSITE: A battered fife-and-drum regiment accompanies Continental troops into battle while a soldier lies wounded in the field. The fifes (small flutes) and drums provided music for marching; signaled troops to assemble, attack, or retreat; and announced daily activities and sounded alarms in camp. Fife-and-drum corps were used by the British Army as well, and their sound has become part of military history.

ask it for money, which the states were free to give or refuse. The central government also had no power to oversee foreign trade.

Many Americans began to call for a new government with more power. The United States had just fought long and hard to gain independence, but now many of its citizens worried that without a new and stronger central government, the United States would crumble. The United States government appeared weak not only to Americans but to leaders of other nations, who were watching the new nation closely to see how the great experiment in freedom and democracy would work out. Some of those countries, particularly European powers, began to believe that the Confederation government was so weak that it would not survive and that they could then take over the United States state by state.

democracy—a form of government in which a majority of votes determines who is elected to office and what laws are passed

Reframing the Government

In 1787, Congress called a meeting in Philadelphia to discuss making changes to the Articles of Confederation. Five delegates from Delaware attended the Constitutional Convention. They were Richard Bassett, Gunning Bedford, Jr., Jacob Broom, John Dickinson, and George Read. The Delaware legislature instructed the delegates to agree to the new document only if it continued to provide each state with only one vote in Congress. As in the past, Delaware was concerned that the large states might gain more voting power than the small ones.

After some discussion, it became clear to the delegates that instead of revising the Articles, the time had come to write an entirely new constitution. The United States was a kind of experiment—a group of states, each with its own democratic form of government, but also with one central democratic government that oversaw the individual states. During the debates, the delegates from Delaware agreed that the central government should be stronger and have more power to make laws. But they did not go along with the plan proposed by the Virginia delegates, who wanted the new constitution to require that the number of votes given to each state in the new national legislature would be based on the state's population. This is called proportional representation and meant that states with large populations would have more votes than states with small populations.

Money printed by individual colonies lost its value after the Revolutionary War when the U.S. Constitution provided that there be one currency for the whole United States.

This issue was debated at the convention for some time. John Dickinson suggested that the new Congress be made up of two sections, or houses, called the Senate and the House of Representatives. Then Roger Sherman from Connecticut proposed that the House should have proportional representation while the Senate should have equal representation, with two senators from each state. The delegates agreed to that proposal, which is now called the Great Compromise.

On September 15, 1787, after debating various issues for almost four months, the delegates approved the new U.S. Constitution. On September 20, the Constitution was presented to Congress. On September 29, Congress voted to present the Constitution to the states for ratification. The delegates to the convention had decided that for the Constitution to become official, nine of the thirteen states had to ratify it.

Delaware Ratifies the Constitution

The Delaware legislature had little doubt that the new Constitution framed a government that would work well. Delaware's president at the time, Thomas Collins, said that ratification of the Constitution was *"a subject of the most important consideration, involving in its adoption not only our prosperity and felicity [happiness], but perhaps our national existence."*

The legislature organized a meeting to take place at Dover on December 3, 1787, during which it would discuss ratification. Each of the three counties was told to select ten delegates to attend. For years, Delaware had struggled to become independent. As a colony it had no "real" name like the other Colonies. It was called the Three Lower Counties, or just the Lower Counties, or the Counties Along the Delaware. In 1776, it became the State of Delaware, and now that state gained a new nickname. On December 7, 1787, Delaware proudly became the first state to ratify the Constitution. It is now known as the First State.

This 1780 painting shows the Cape Henlopen lighthouse that marked the entrance to Delaware Bay for more than 150 years. The spit of land on which it stood has been a silent witness to Delaware's history, guiding colonists, merchants, and warships from the open ocean to the protected shores of the bay and river beyond.

Time Line

1602 The Dutch East India Company is chartered and sponsors exploration to expand overseas trade.

1609 Henry Hudson, attempting to find a western route to the East Indies, sails into Delaware Bay.

1610 Samuel Argall explores the Delaware coastline.

1621 The Dutch West India Company is formed.

1631 The Dutch settle Zwaanendael.

1632 Captain David Pieterson de Vries sails with new colonists to Zwaanendael and discovers that all the inhabitants have been killed and the buildings burned.

1638 Peter Minuit establishes New Sweden with Swedish and Finnish settlers.

1642 The Swedish government takes over the New Sweden Company.

1651 The Dutch begin their attempt to take over New Sweden and build Fort Kasimier, just south of Fort Christina.

1653 Johan Printz, governor of New Sweden, returns to Holland.

1654 Johan Rising replaces Printz and forces the Dutch at Fort Kasimier to surrender.

1655 The Dutch take over New Sweden. Their rule lasts until 1664.

1664 Sir Robert Carr claims the land for James, Duke of York. The area is now an English colony, called the Three Lower Counties along the Delaware.

1681 The Duke of York turns over the Lower Counties to William Penn.

1701 Welsh leaders are granted 30,000 acres (12,000 ha), around Iron Hill.

1704 Penn grants the Lower Counties a separate legislature, and New Castle becomes their colonial capital.

1731 Thomas Willing founds Wilmington.

1742 Oliver Canby builds the first of many flour mills along the Brandywine River.

1748 Wilmington Friends School is founded by Quakers.

1765 The Wilmington Academy is given a charter. Caesar Rodney and Thomas McKean represent the Lower Counties at the Stamp Act Congress.

1768 The survey for the Mason-Dixon Line is completed, setting the boundaries between Maryland and Pennsylvania, and later, Delaware.

1774 The Lower Counties send aid to Boston; Rodney, McKean, and George Read represent the Lower Counties at the First Continental Congress.

1775 The Lower Counties form militias and raise at least 5,000 men.

1776 The Lower Counties, now called Delaware, declare themselves not only free from Britain but also separate from Pennsylvania; on July 1–2 Rodney makes a historic overnight ride from Dover to Philadelphia to cast the vote that puts Delaware on the side of independence. Delaware adopts its first state constitution.

1777 Dover becomes the state capital; on September 3 British and American troops skirmish at Coochs Bridge; the British occupy Wilmington until October.

1781 The British surrender at Yorktown, ending the war.

1787 On December 7, Delaware becomes the first state to ratify the U.S. Constitution.

Resources

BOOKS

Blashfield, Jean F. *Delaware (America the Beautiful).* Danbury, CT.: Children's Press, 2000.

Cheripko, Jan. *Caesar Rodney's Ride: The Story of an American Patriot.* Honesdale, PA.: Boyds Mills Press, 2004.

Dubois, Muriel L. *The Delaware Colony (Fact Finders: The American Colonies.* Mankato, MN: Capstone Press, 2005.

Fradin, Dennis B. *The Delaware Colony (Thirteen Colonies).* Danbury, CT: Children's Press, 1992.

Wilker, Josh. *The Lenape Indians (Junior Library of American Indians).* Broomall, PA.: Chelsea House, 1994.

Worth, Richard. *Life in the Thirteen Colonies: Delaware.* Danbury, CT.: Children's Press, 2004.

WEB SITES

Delaware Tribe of Indians
http://www.delawaretribeofindians.nsn.us/

Facts for Kids: Lenape Indian Fact Sheet
http://www.geocities.com/bigorrin/lenape_kids.htm

History of Delaware for Kids
http://www.state.de.us/gic/facts/history/delhist.htm

The *Kalmar Nyckel*
http://www.kalmarnyckel.org/

State of Delaware
http://www.state.de.us/gic/facts/history/delhist.htm

Quote Sources

CHAPTER ONE

Chapter One
p. 23 "We understood...working the land." Morgan, Michael. Delaware Diary, Hidden in the Soil. http://www.deldot.net/static/projects/archaeology/articles/dd-hidden_in_the_soil_5-4-05-cp.pdf; "skulls...with them." Morgan; pp. 23–24 "those in command...like again." Ashmead, Henry. *History of Delaware County, Pennsylvania.* Philadelphia: L.H. Everts & Co., 1884, p. 3 of Chapter II online: http://www.delcohistory.org/ashmead/ashmead_pg3.htm; "Observing our people...fell down dead."Ashmead, p. 3 of Chapter II online; p. 27 "who had...such offence." Ashmead, p. 4 of Chapter II online; "It was after...on board." Scharf, Thomas J. *History of Delaware, 1609–1888.* Philadelphia: L.J. Richards & Co. 1888, http://www.accessible.com/amcnty/DE/Delaware/delaware5.htm; p. 28 "dozens of...for the Indians." *Immigrants to New Netherland: 1637 in the* Kalmar Nickel. http://www.rootsweb.com/~nycoloni/shcs.html; p. 29 "to send over...now possess." Hoffecker, Carol E. *Delaware: A Bicentennial History.* New York: W.W. Norton & Company, Inc., 1977, p. 17.

CHAPTER TWO

p. 35 "an empty...we still prosper." *Report of Governor Johan Rising, 1654.* http://www.libraries.psu.edu/digital/pahistory/liz_pdfs/rising.pdf; p. 136; "in order...return cargo." pp. 139–140; p. 36 "The Christina... milk and honey." Hoffecker, Carol E. *Delaware: A Bicentennial History.* New York: W.W. Norton & Company, Inc., 1977, p. 16.; p. 41 "join and...our government." http://www.delcohistory.org/ashmead/ashmead_pg11.htm, par. 2.

CHAPTER FOUR

p. 63 "The times within...and chocolate." Scharf, Thomas J. *History of Delaware, 1609–1888.* Philadelphia: L.J. Richards & Co., 1888, http://www.accessible.com/amcnty/DE/Delaware/delaware13.htm, par. 41.

CHAPTER FIVE

p. 71 "These colonies...the Stamp Act." http://vcehistory.info/pdf/adoc8.pdf, par. 3.

CHAPTER SIX

p. 78 "these United...independent states." "Journals of the Continental Congress, Resolution of Richard Henry Lee; June 7, 1776." The Avalon Project at Yale Law School, http://www.yale.edu/lawweb/avalon/contcong/06-07-76.htm, par. 10; p. 79 "I arrived...independence." "Caesar Rodney to Thomas Rodney, July 4, 1776." *Letters of delegates to Congress, 1774–1789, Volume 4, May 16, 1776–August 15, 1776.* Electronic Text Center, University of Virginia Library. http://etext.virginia.edu/etcbin/toccer-new2?id=DelVol04.xml&images=images/modeng&data=/texts/english/modeng/parsed&t ag=public&part=302&division=div1, letter 306; p. 81 "The Delaware... wish to See." "Caesar Rodney to Thomas Rodney, July 4, 1776." *Letters of delegates to Congress, 1774–1789, Volume 4, May 16 1776–August 15 1776.* Electronic Text Center, University of Virginia Library. http://etext.virginia.edu/etcbin/toccer-new2?id=DelVol04.xml&images=images/modeng&data=/texts/english/modeng/parsed&tag=public&part=302&division=div1 letter 549; p. 85 "The Congress... can be done." "Historical Society of Delaware—George Washington Letter." http://hsd.org/washington_letter.htm, paragraph 1.

CHAPTER SEVEN

p. 88 "I could not...encampment." "Elk Neck, Maryland." http://www.revolutionaryday.com/usroute202/elkneck/default.htm, par. 5; "a beautiful...August sun." "The Philadelphia Campaign 1777: On the March to Brandywine, Part 1 of 10—Moving on Up." http://www.ushistory.org/march/phila/tobrandywine_1.htm, par. 4; p. 92 "We are Constantly...Houses plundered." Scott, Jane Harrington. *A Gentleman as Well as a Whig: Caesar Rodney and the American Revolution.* Newark: University of Delaware Press, 2000, p. 174; pp. 92–93 "The people...of provisions." Hoffecker, Carol E. *Delaware: A Bicentennial History.* New York: W.W. Norton & Company, Inc., 1977, p.166; p. 94 "I can...their works." www.doverpost.com/PostArchives/07-03-02/pages/kentfarm.html, par. 10; p. 95 "what is yet...[wretched] enemy." Turner, Rev. Joseph Brown, editor. *The Journal and Order Book of Captain Robert Kirkwood of the Delaware Regiment of the Continental Line. Part II: An Order Book of the Campaign in New Jersey, 1777.* Wilmington: The Historical Society of Delaware, 1910, pp. 65–66; "Francis War...future orders." Turner, p. 79; p. 96 "The shorter...skilful training." Scott, p. 198; p. 97 "I set out...the inhabitants." Edward W. Cooch, Lt. Governor, sponsor. *Delaware: A Guide to the First State.* New York: The Viking Press, 1938, p. 182.

CHAPTER EIGHT

p. 102 "a subject of...national existence." Munroe, John. A. *Federalist Delaware: 1775–1815.* New Brunswick, NJ: Rutgers University Press, 1954, p. 108.

INDEX

Boldface indicates illustrations.

About the Author and Consultant

KAREN HOSSELL is the author of more than 40 nonfiction books for middle grade and high school readers. Topics she has written about include key American documents and historic events, early European explorers, biographies of famous Americans, colonial America, geography and mapping, and methods of communication. This is her first book for National Geographic. She lives in Winter Park, Florida.

KARIN WULF is an associate professor of history and American studies at the College of William and Mary in Williamsburg, Virginia. She earned her Ph.D. from Johns Hopkins University and writes frequently about the Mid-Atlantic region of colonial America. Wulf is the book review editor of the *William and Mary Quarterly*. She was also the consultant for *Voices from Colonial America: Pennsylvania* and lives in Rockville, Maryland.

Illustration Credits

Cover: Courtesy of the Historical Society of Delaware

End sheets, pages 8, 59, 98: The Library of Congress

Title page, pages 19, 23, 30, 47, 54, 63: Picture Collection, The Branch Libraries, The New York Public Library, Astor, Lenox and Tilden Foundation

Pages 8 (inset), 38, 57: National Geographic

Pages 9, 16, 33, 49, 71, 76, 84, 86, 101, 103: Courtesy of the Historical Society of Delaware

Page 11: Getty Images

Pages 12, 40 72: Bridgeman Art Library

Pages 21, 36, 42, 45, 50, 60, 66, 69, 81, 89, 93: The Granger Collection

Pages 26, 35, 53, 79, 90: North Wind Picture Archives

Page 62: Delaware Public Archives

Page 74: Art Resource

Page 76: Collections of Delaware Division of Historical and Cultural Affairs

Page 84: State Portrait Collection, Delaware Division of Historical and Cultural Affairs

NORTH AMERICA Divided into its III PRINCIPALL PARTS 1st ENGLISH Part Viz ENGLISH EMPIRE containin
N Foundland N Scotland N England N York N Jarsey Pensylvania Maryland Virginia Carolina Carolania or Florida California, Sommer Is Bahama Is Jamaica & ye Caribby Is II SPANISH Pt viz N S

1685

BAFFINS BAY

ARCTICK

NEW NORTH WALES

NEW SOUTH WALES

HUDS

L. PISCOUTAGAMI

L. TABITIBIS

LAKE SUPERIOR

LAKE HURONS

ILINOIS

Tract of Land full of Wild Bulls

NEW ALBION

CALIFORNIA

SEA OF CALIFORNIA

MAR VERMEIO

NEW MEXICO

New Mexico

NEW BISCAIA

ZACATECAS

THE GOLF OR BAY OF MEXICO

Fort St George

YUCATAN

HONDURAS

SEA OF NEW SPAIN